Pursuit of Passion

Pursuit of Passion

DISCOVERING TRUE INTIMACY
IN YOUR MARRIAGE

Jeff & Glynis Murphy • *Randall & Julie Sibert*

ISBN 13: 9780991129423
ISBN: 0991129423

1st ed. - 1

1. Marriage-Sex. 2. Sex - Biblical teaching. 3. Marriage-Religious aspects-Christianity.

We dedicate this book to…

Young adults growing up in a world that has lost sight of God's best for their lives and marriages...

Those to whom we have the privilege of mentoring and ministering to regarding their marriages and relationships...

Pastors, counselors and marriage mentors who are teaching people God's truth…

Those who have blessed our lives through instruction, wise counsel and godly example – inspiring us to build marriages that are fulfilling and a great source of joy…

And those in the Church-at-Large who have been longing for someone to tell them the whole truth about sexual intimacy.

Introduction

§

SOME OF YOU READING THIS book may not be accustomed to detailed coverage of the topic of sex from a biblical perspective. Maybe you grew up in a home or attended a church where discussing sex was handled with such awkwardness that you got the message loud and clear, "We don't talk about *that* around here."

We've been there too, and we understand what you have been through. In this book we have tried to be honest, direct and unashamed in presenting what we believe are God's views on sex. In areas that the Bible specifically addresses, we gladly accept His wisdom and truth. In areas where God is silent, we seek to apply biblical principles as we glean the most reliable information from the medical and social sciences that do not contradict Scripture. But since sex is such a "hot-button" topic, you may find some points that, even after you have prayed about them, you still choose not agree with us. That's okay. Hopefully, you will find many other points that resonate deeply with you and are refreshingly helpful.

In our world, so much is being said and done with sex that it's become commonplace and has lost its Divine meaning and mystery. Casual sex, hookups, booty calls and pornography have become the painful norm for so many people. Sexual purity, which was once widely accepted without question, has now become something that is routinely subjected to mockery and scorn.

In the church, sex is hardly discussed at all, as if the topic should be shrouded in a veil of secrecy and shame. Both extremes have led to another generation that has knowledge about sex, but often without a clear understanding of the proper context for truly awesome sex.

The painful consequences of the dramatic cultural shift in secular world view continue to mount. So much of what couples experience sexually is focused on the physical aspects of attraction alone. Surgically enhanced hot bodies are displayed like idols at a pagan temple. But there is a LOT more going on behind the scenes and between the sheets when it comes to sex. If sex was only physical, we would just be copulating animals, but God created us to be much more than that.

Consider the world around you. Look up at the sun, moon and stars. When we look at the beauty, variety and splendor of God's creation, we catch a glimpse of His character, power and wisdom. No one can miss noticing it. Psalm 19:1-3 tells us,

"The heavens declare the glory of God; the skies proclaim the work of his hands. Day after day they pour forth speech; night after night they reveal knowledge. They have no speech, they use no words; no sound is heard from them."

Love also is the work of God's hand, for God is love (1 John 4:8). Marital love, with sex at the core of marriage, is an incredible exchange between a husband and a wife, which involves not only a physical response but an emotional and spiritual response as well. God designed sex to be that way! It's the highest form of whole-person connection and was designed to reflect the deep love that Jesus Christ has for His Church (Ephesians 5:32). It's a sacred act, set apart to be experienced within the context of a covenant marriage. In that setting alone, sex reflects Christ and the Church.

We wrote this book to help couples form a healthy, balanced and biblically sound view of sex and to fully experience what God designed for their marriage. In this book we will explore sex from a variety of perspectives, including:

- How to develop healthy expectations regarding sex
- The purposes of sex
- How to enhance desire and arousal
- Techniques that help couples orgasm
- How to have healthy communication about sex
- Ways to handle struggles and differences in desire
- Working together successfully for a lifetime of sexual fulfillment.

When a couple's sex life is going well, it contributes about 20 percent to overall feelings of marital satisfaction and intimacy. When things aren't going so well in the bedroom, sexual frustration can drain the marriage of 50 to 75 percent of its intimacy.

Our ultimate desire is that after reading this book, you would be sexually fulfilled and that your marriage would bring greater glory to God. After all, sex was God's idea. He could have designed it however He wanted to, but He chose to also include within sex, boundless potential for passion, pleasure, mystery and oneness. Far more than a mere side note, sex is meant to strengthen and enrich your marriage in such a unique and profound way. When viewed in this light, who wouldn't want to do all they can to nurture God's idea? That's exactly what we hope you will do!

Whether you had sex before you were married or you were a virgin on your wedding day, we are confident this book is for you.

Who better than two mature Christian couples who are enthusiastic about this topic of sexual intimacy to provide insights that could be so beneficial to your marriage? We encourage you to read this book together as a couple. Use it as a springboard for generating authentic conversations about sex and your marriage. Don't be bashful. You won't regret it.

We would love to hear how this book has impacted you and your marriage. Feel free to share your thoughts on Twitter @PursuitOPassion, Facebook (http://facebook.com/pursuitofpassion) or write to us at authors@pursuitofpassionbook.com. While we may not be able to reply to all emails individually, we do read them all and will address frequently raised issues through our social media sites.

Table of Contents

CHAPTER 1

Why a Book on Sex for Christians?

§

WHETHER YOU ARE ENGAGED OR recently married, you are eagerly anticipating your life together as husband and wife, right? Of course you are!

Like most couples early in their marital journey, you are in love and want a strong and healthy marriage – not just now, but for decades.

We want that for you too! That's why we are glad you are reading this book. It may be difficult to wrap your mind around this truth right now, but we encourage you to trust us on it: God wants the very best for your marriage, and sexual intimacy is absolutely vital in building that kind of marriage.

You can get your marriage off to the right start sexually. You can foster passionate sexual intimacy that is not only mutually enjoyable but also sustains your relationship in unfathomable ways.

We wrote this book to help show you how to do precisely that. You do not have to follow the world's practices regarding sex or the patterns of other married Christians who have neglected or under-estimated the value of nurtured intimacy.

You may wonder, "But what if we already had sex, either with each other or with others, before we were married? Is this book still for us?"

Yes! Even if you had sex before you were married (as many Christians have), you will find this book extremely beneficial as you now seek to build phenomenal sexual intimacy in your marriage.

We have found that many married couples struggle with address-ing and healing from their past sexual promiscuity, and this lack of healing begins to take a toll on their marriage. They sometimes erroneously think past sexual sin is beyond the forgiveness of Jesus, or they go the other route and allow past sexual experiences to skew how they view sex with their spouse. If any of those scenarios sound familiar, rest assured that sex in your marriage does not have to be defined by sex in your past. We will show you how.

After mentoring engaged and married couples for the past 13 years, we (Glynis and Jeff) have seen many couples struggling with is-sues in this area of their relationships. In most cases, prudishness has given way to permissiveness, and the sexual issues Christian couples often face include pornography addiction, compulsive masturbation, infidelity, sexual abuse, "mismatched" sexual desire, and emotional scars and guilt from sexual sin. Underlying patterns stood out in the lives of many of our mentees that initially surprised us. These in-dividuals and couples typically came from strong Christian homes, professed faith in Jesus Christ, attended evangelical churches, and rarely, if ever, heard sexuality spoken about in a positive, biblical and comprehensive way at home or in church.

As a consequence of growing up in an environment where sex was rarely discussed by those who could have had a positive influence in their lives, our mentees' views and actions were largely shaped by a valueless educational system, media and culture that has virtually hijacked the discussion of sex. Missing from their understanding and relationships was a clear, biblical view of sex as a beautiful gift from our loving God who designed marital love to be pleasurable, passionate, pure, intimate and His chosen illustration to teach us about of His love for His people (Ephesians 5:32). They also were never taught how to bring maximum sexual pleasure to each other once married.

As we incorporated more on the topic of sex into our mentoring sessions, couples consistently responded with a combination of excitement, relief and gratitude. Comments from young men often included, "Wow, I never heard that before. I can't thank you enough for what you just did for me," and young women frequently responded with, "Thanks for answering my questions honestly and biblically. I could never have asked my mom these questions that I had."

In contrast to those positive responses, we have encountered both an awkward discomfort and overt resistance from some church leaders regarding our inclusion of sex education in our mentoring. Sadly, this resistance took place even while many of their members, who approached us requesting our comprehensive marriage and premarriage mentoring, were struggling with a variety of hidden sexual sins. The church's silence had left these individuals with a void in their understanding of the sacredness of sex and the perception that sex was indeed something shameful and best not talked about. The resulting isolation left them trapped in their sexual sins and struggling to fight on their own.

Perhaps this unfounded resistance came from the leader's own personal struggles with sexual sin or a fear that speaking openly about sex and sexual pleasure would stir up greater temptation for single people. But what we have found is that once people fully understand the sacred beauty of sex, their desire to obey God's Word in this area of their lives greatly increases. Several of our mentee couples actually asked us to hold them accountable to sexual purity, and they are now enjoying victory over sexual sin for the first time in their lives.

When I (Julie) began writing and speaking on sexual intimacy in marriage, I also discovered that many Christians were struggling in silence with sexual matters. Those struggles run the gamut from infidelity and pornography addiction to issues with sexual infrequency in marriage to miscommunication about sexual expectations.

Regardless of the struggles, a common thread is an extreme hesitancy of many Christians to seek godly counsel and resources. In some regards, the church – the body of believers – carries some of the responsibility for this silence. We, as Christians, generally are uncomfortable talking about sex – let alone talking in specifics about sexual pleasure, struggles and solutions. It's as if we have the mentality that if we don't talk about sex, young people won't engage in it or sexual problems for married couples will somehow disappear.

Some courageous Christians are now generating more authentic conversation about sexual intimacy. More books are being written, and more marriage ministries are being started. Some pastors and church leaders are not only broaching the topic more often but are also offering valuable godly information that is helping married couples nurture their intimacy and, in some cases, save their marriages. We applaud those leaders!

Our intention is that you will fully grasp that the Holy Spirit desires that you welcome Him into every part of your life, including your sexual intimacy. His desire is that every expression of your sexuality would be pleasing to your Heavenly Father and be all that He designed your sexual relationship to represent. Anyone can choose to live a sexually pure and faithful life, but only a Christian can represent Christ and His Church, and in doing so, delight the heart of God.

Sex Is God's Idea

Where did you first learn about sex? Often this information was obtained through some combination of embarrassed parents; a health or biology teacher; teammates in a locker room; friends at a sleepover; or from movies, magazines and the Internet. What we typically glean from these sources can be a potentially dangerous collection of half-truths and misinformation, and certainly little understanding of the fact that God designed sex to be an incredibly pleasurable experience for a husband and wife. We see the unfortunate results of this haphazard approach to "sex education" in the majority of engaged and married Christian couples whom we mentor.

What do you think about sex? If you are married, is it something you enjoy and look forward to, or is it something you dread or endure? Is it always at the bottom of your "To-Do" list or near the top? Has sex become routine and boring, or does it still send chills through your body?

Stop for a moment and think about it. Sex is God's idea – not ours. When God finished His work creating the first man and woman having designed them to become one flesh sexually, He declared that this was "very good" (Genesis 1:31). That being the case, isn't it reasonable to expect that a loving God would give us the instructions and principles to apply for the maximum fulfillment and enjoyment of sex? Shouldn't our sexual experiences, if done God's way, be filled with blessing, joy and fulfillment?

Consider this. We live in an age where Satan, whom the Bible calls "the god of this world" (2 Corinthians 4:4), is seeking to destroy our lives, our marriages and our families (1 Peter 5:8). Satan's go-to method is division, and he will use whatever means possible to divide a husband and wife because their intimate marriage is a covenant relationship designed by God. What God meant for good – in this case, sex – Satan goes to great lengths to skew, manipulate and destroy.

We see the evidence of this destruction whenever we encounter cases of sexual abuse; the degradation of both men and women through pornography; the rampant spread of STDs; distorted views of marriage; unhealthy and immoral sexual practices; and sexual, emotional and spiritual brokenness. (If you were sexually abused or experienced any other sexual trauma in your past, we encourage you to read Chapter 13 first.)

We are living in an age where the "experts" in our culture are promoting valueless, incomplete and incorrect information regarding sex and human sexuality. Rarely is God's design for sex even considered, and if it is, that view is often lacking in accuracy and comprehensiveness or it is portrayed as "boring" or mere duty.

Societal messages seem to scream, "All the fun sex is happening among singles and 'friends with benefits'!" Married sex, on the other hand? Well, that's fodder for comedy in sitcoms or jokes on late night talk shows.

Today, Christian couples are desperate for honest, truthful, biblically sound information about sex. In our rapidly changing culture, moral values that were once upheld without question are being challenged from every direction and are being discarded without regard for the consequences that people are experiencing. Pastors and Christian leaders in many cases have been left behind in the discussion of sex and that void has been filled by media "stars" promoting non-biblical views. We've let the world "hijack" the conversation.

If you want remarkable sex, you will have to develop a discerning eye and heart to steer clear of society's casual sex message and follow the instructions from your Creator.

Answering the question, "What is 'God's way' when it comes to sex?" is the reason why we wrote this book. In it, we openly and honestly discuss topics that are important for you to understand in order to have not just a healthy sex life, but a passionate and intensely pleasurable one too. God's plan for sex is wonderful, so there's no need for any shame or awkwardness. Let it go!

To get started, let's look at the big picture and review a historical perspective of sex and the church. We'll try to keep this section interesting, but if history bores you, feel free to skip over to the "Going Deeper Together" section at the end of this chapter.

WHY SO MUCH CONFUSION?

You may wonder, "Why does it even matter what Christians thought or taught about sex long ago? Shouldn't we just be concentrating on sex in our marriage now?" We hear what you're saying, but at the same time, you might be surprised that understanding the past can better equip you to understand and navigate the present and the future. Many of the struggles that Christians have with sex are rooted in skewed information from long ago. The historical relationship between the church and sexuality has been quite tense.

> *"The problem isn't that people know too little, but that people know too much that just ain't so."*

> ~ MARK TWAIN

In fact, there's been a lot of misinformation on sex from the church! We want you equipped to embrace God's vision for sexual intimacy in your marriage. It may be easier to do that if you see that Christians – even well-meaning ones – have at times been wrong in their teachings about sex. This wrong teaching can be traced back to the influence on the early church by prominent ascetic philosophers who taught that there was a conflict between the evil mortal body and the good immortal soul. *Ascetic* is simply a scholarly word for "those who practice extreme self-denial, renounce material possessions and abstain from all forms of physical pleasure which they view as inherently evil."

2ᴺᴰ ᴛᴏ 5ᵀᴴ Cᴇɴᴛᴜʀʏ

During this time period, ascetic thinking stood in stark contrast to the prevailing ancient Greek and Roman mindset that promoted every imaginable form of free sexual expression. The ascetics found an open ear among some prominent early church leaders and had great influence on their views regarding sex, physical pleasure and eventually, celibacy. Here are some examples.

Tertullian (155-220 A.D.) and Ambrose (340-397 A.D.) preferred the end of the human race to continued sexual activity. Origen (185-254 A.D.) thought that sex was so evil that he allegorized the Song of Songs (also known as Song of Solomon) and is believed to have castrated himself to assure that he would never experience sexual pleasure!

Jerome (347-420 A.D.) declared that,

"...all sexual intercourse is unclean. As regards to Adam and Eve we must maintain that before the fall they were virgins in Paradise; but after they sinned, and were cast out of Paradise, they were immediately married."[1]

Jerome's conclusion surely sounds strange, especially when you consider that God named the garden in which He placed Adam and Eve *Eden*, which means "pleasure and delight."

Augustine (354-430 A.D.) – In his book on Western sexual morality, C. W. Lloyd says,

"Augustine's writings have probably exerted more influence in the West on love and sexual practice than those of any other man." As the leading theologian of the 4th century, Augustine considered the 'forbidden fruit' in Genesis to be symbolic for sex and commended couples for not having sex. He was an early proponent of the church's 'marriage law' that viewed sex as being solely for procreation, stating, '... *that which goes beyond this necessity [begetting children] no longer follows reason but lust.*'"[2]

In other words, unless procreation was the intent, sex was to be avoided. Augustine believed that people should not only abstain from sex but avoid even *thinking* about sex.

James Brundage says in *Law, Sex, and Christian Society in Medieval Europe,*

"*Sexual relations within marriage were a good use of an evil thing. Virginity, to be sure, was better, since that was a good use of a good thing. While marital relations were also good, they constituted a lesser order of good, because they employed the intrinsic wickedness of sex to achieve a morally valuable good.*"[3]

This thinking entrenched an anti-sexual bias in the church and led to Catholic priests being forbidden to marry – a policy that continues to this day.

6ᵗʰ TO 15ᵗʰ CENTURY – THE MIDDLE AGES

Throughout the Middle Ages, the church's interest in sex focused on controlling what was going on within marriages, including when couples could have sex. *Penitentials*, "books containing long lists of sins and their associated penance," were written to communicate church policy. Sex was not allowed during pregnancy or menstruation, after the birth of a child, during Lent which could last from one and a half to two months, on certain feast days, or before communion. Some priests recommended abstinence for married couples covering five of the seven days of the week. Priests not only began telling people when they could have sex but also what positions they could use. Only one was allowed – the "Missionary position," with the husband on top, face-to-face with his wife.[4]

Upon marrying, a couple could not enter a church for 30 days.[5]

Drawing upon church tradition, Thomas Aquinas (1225-1274 A.D.) reiterated that sex was only permissible for making babies and saw sexual abstinence as superior to marriage. While he didn't view marital relations as being necessarily contaminated by lust, he regretted that sexual pleasure involved letting go of one's self- control.

16TH TO 21ST CENTURY

16TH TO 21ST CENTURY

Protestant Reformation leaders such as Calvin and Luther maintained many of the traditional views on sex but rejected clerical celibacy, and each eventually got married. They also viewed sexual pleasure in marriage as being natural and morally proper, as long as it didn't degenerate into lust.

Others, like the Quakers, viewed sex as a gift from God that wasn't essentially good or evil. They viewed sex as a normal human activity in which people indulge either creatively or destructively through selfish desires.[6]

Whew! Much of this church history has long since been forgotten, but it still wields some influence on the church even today. While we do glance back and see some positive attitudes about sexual purity, the church as a whole doesn't have a good track record on conveying biblical truth about sexuality and intimacy. Skewed and downright wrong theology by some early church leaders set a shaky foundation for continued misguided attempts to deal with this topic of sexual intimacy.

Today, across various Protestant denominations, there are many divergent views regarding human sexuality. Thankfully, some come from Scripture and are liberating for couples. Unfortunately, other prevailing teachings that are rooted in church traditions continue to deprive married couples of the blessings that God intended.

What can we learn from this historical perspective?

Like an ocean tide, the ebb and flow of secular thought is ever changing. In many ways, this secular thought has also been an unreliable source for truth and direction for a person's life. Even within Christianity, views are once again being influenced by the prevailing secular culture, only this time that pull is toward sexual permissiveness.

We can look back at history to gain greater perspective and to learn from past mistakes. Otherwise, we are likely to repeat those mistakes and make more of our own. What lessons can we learn from the historical church?

1. Even when we have a relationship with God through Jesus Christ, the influence of the culture in which we live colors our views, often in ways that are barely discernible at the

time. It is only in taking God at His word and viewing things through the lens of Scripture that we have a chance of breaking free from our cultural norms.

2. God's Word provides us with the only reliable source of wisdom and truth. When we add to it or make it out to be something other than what God intended, it says more about who we are than about who God is.

3. God is love (1 John 4:8), and He loves us enough not to leave us wandering through life and marriage blindly. God has given us instructions regarding sex to protect us from both Satan and ourselves. He has provided us with a roadmap, a set of boundaries for our protection, and forgiveness that brings healing from the pain of our past and opens up a whole new opportunity for true fulfillment in our marriage.

4. While many times we need to rein in our fleshly desires, there are also times when we need to let go of legalism and embrace greater sexual freedom in our marriage. God is a whole lot more comfortable with the idea of sex and sexual pleasure than most of us are. Understanding that fact can be truly liberating for your marriage.

When we really start to peel back the layers and dig into God's Word, we find He has a lot to say about sex. Sadly, the church has tended to lean heavy on "what not to do" – admonishment particularly to young people. Lost has been a balanced approach that gives equal time to speaking boldly and authentically in favor of nurtured sexual intimacy in marriage.

A lot of misinformation is still going around and Christian couples aren't immune from the consequence – sexual brokenness. *It's time for the Church to engage couples in the conversation!*

We realize that a book like this will be met with mixed reactions both within and outside the church. While we wish that were not the case, it's impossible to write a meaningful book about sex without that happening.

Unfortunately, some church leaders will continue to let the culture hijack the conversation about sex through their silence. Their members have been left with the choice of suffering in silence or turning to those outside the church for answers and guidance.

Thankfully, we also have seen pastors embrace sexuality as a gift from God, stay in touch with what is going on in the church and culture, and unashamedly teach what their flock needs to learn. We applaud such courage and leadership.

With *Pursuit of Passion: Discovering True Intimacy in Your Marriage*, all Christian couples, pastors and counselors now have a new option for helping couples deal with their sexual questions and concerns from a biblical and practical perspective, and equipping them to experience all that God designed for them sexually.

We encourage you to glean from this book what is applicable to your marriage and use it to motivate yourself toward incredible sexual connection with each other.

GOING DEEPER TOGETHER

1. How did you each initially learn about sex? Was the information you received accurate and appropriate for your age? Is there anything you wish you would have been told that you weren't?

2. How do you think the church or other Christians influenced your view of sex? What about society and/or culture?
3. In what ways would you each like to grow sexually as individuals and as a couple? How do you think that would benefit your marriage?

CHAPTER 2

A Biblical View of Sex and Marriage

§

*"Most teaching on sex inside the church is inadequate,
and most teaching on it outside the church is perverted."*

~ MARK & GRACE DRISCOLL, AUTHORS OF THE BOOK *REAL MARRIAGE*

SEX IS BOTH "LESS" THAN the myth we have made it out to be and *more* than we could ever imagine! How can that be?

LESS MYTH

Let me (Jeff) tell you a story. When I was a teenager, my brother and I collected coins as a hobby. There was a rare penny that we dreamed of owning one day, the 1877 Indian Cent. At the time, that one cent piece in very fine condition was worth about $100. When we went to coin shows, we would often gaze at that coin in a dealer's display case and sometimes even ask to hold it, looking forward to the day when we could purchase one just like it.

After saving for about a year, we were able to finally buy one for our collection. I remember looking at it countless times during our first few months of ownership and then putting it away for safe storage, where it remained for a few decades.

As we grew older our interests changed, and we decided it was time to sell the coin to another collector. We were thrilled to find that this coin was now worth over $1,500, so we listed it for sale. The bids started coming in, and we soon found a buyer. After receiving payment, we mailed the coin to its new owner.

And then reality hit us.

We received a note back from the buyer informing us that this coin, which we had proudly admired, had been determined by the American Numismatic Association to be counterfeit! Not only was it *not* worth $1,500, it wasn't even worth one cent! For decades we had believed that we had the "real deal," while unknowingly we had fallen for a counterfeit.

Sex can be like that too.

We live in a hypersexualized world. Whenever you view media in any form, you likely encounter sexuality elevated to a god-like status. Hollywood actors are routinely featured in glamorously provocative poses while we are subtly brainwashed to believe that we don't measure up to those "beautiful people." We begin to think that if we want to be valued by others, we need to look more like the famous people by losing weight, changing our hair style or wearing the latest fashions in order to be just as "sexy." Otherwise, we will have to settle for being single or having a boring life as – gasp – a married person.

We've made an art form out of idolizing youthfulness, unbridled sexuality and surgically enhanced "beauty" that's about as real as plastic fruit. So much of the entertainment industry is built upon myths about sex, love and beauty. In the movies, two beautiful people meet and within minutes they are tearing off their clothes, having mind-blowing, passionate sex, complete with simultaneous orgasms. Having met their "soul mate," they are now destined for a life filled with love and endless fulfillment. Even "reality" programming is manipulated and fabricated in such a way that we easily buy into this idea that all the truly great sex and love happens to *other* people – and when it does happen, it's nothing short of perfect and spectacular all of the time.

But in reality, these sexual myths aren't realistic for *anyone.* This Hollywood view of love and sex is rooted in fantasy and infatuation, and separated from the covenant of marriage. Like gasoline on a fire, this view of passion burns intensely for a few moments and then quickly goes out. This can be seen in the serial marriages, some lasting mere days or hours, which are so common among celebrities.

Even when announcing their divorces, the farce often continues with straight-faced celebrities claim that they "still deeply love each other and will continue to be 'great friends.'" Great friends who deeply love each other don't break their marriage commitments. True love doesn't behave that way (1 Corinthians 13:4-8).

Today, we have a surplus of sex in our culture but a deficit of true love and authentic sexual intimacy. It's time to stop pretending that this gold-plated, brass idol of sex is real. God has so much more in mind for you than a cheap counterfeit. His vision of sex in your marriage is deeper and more fulfilling than what the entertainment world portrays. Yes, that's right. His plan for sex will rock your world in ways that are probably hard to imagine right now!

Let's take a look at God's plan for marriage and how sex fits into that plan, for it is God's standards and plans that ultimately protect us from ourselves and simultaneously offer us a path to phenomenal sexual intimacy.

More of Reality

The Bible clearly shows us that sex and marriage are important to God. God's Word begins with a marriage in Eden (Genesis 2:24) where Adam and Eve become one flesh. This marriage is presented as a relationship like no other, with a husband and his wife cleaving – being bonded together – to each other, and becoming one. This relationship was to take priority above all other relationships, except for their relationship with God.

God also devoted an entire book of the Bible – Song of Songs – to the lavish wedding of Solomon and Shulamith, the consummation of their marriage and their ongoing passionate lovemaking. In Song of Songs 5:1, God Himself encourages the couple to become "intoxicated with each other's love." He's not talking about emotionless, boring, mechanical sex in the dark. In Song of Songs, we also read about this couple's discreetly having sex out in the vineyard and in other places. God's plan for married couples included passionate sex *long* before Hollywood came on the scene.

In Proverbs, nothing is vague about the way God contrasts the devastation of sexual sin against the rich significance of marital sex. He goes so far as to tell the husbands to be satisfied by his wife's breasts and captivated by her love (5:19), and exclusively devoted to her sexually (5:15). Marital sex described in that context hardly sounds boring or routine.

God commands husbands and wives to have sex often in 1 Corinthians 7:5, in order to strengthen their marriage bond by not depriving each other sexually. The only conditions given to couples for abstaining are only by mutual consent, for short periods of time and for the purpose of devoting themselves to prayer.

In Ephesians 5:32, the marriage relationship is revealed to be God's chosen representation of the most intimate relationship known – the love between Christ and His Church. This relationship is based on Jesus' coming as a servant and placing our needs ahead of His own (Philippians 2:5-11). This serves as the greatest example for us to seek to emulate in our marriages.

Finally, Revelation 19:6-9 presents us with an extravagant event that awaits believers in Heaven, the ultimate marriage feast that Jesus Christ has prepared for His bride, the Church. Here God puts on the celebration of celebrations and uses a wedding feast to celebrate His great love for His people.

There is a lot for us to learn from God's Word regarding sex. The Bible has many passages that teach husbands and wives how to love each other and develop a great sex life.

Unfortunately, most couples have never experienced what God intended sex to be. Why? For some, it's because of missing or improper teaching or examples. For others, it due to the guilt and consequences of going outside God's design for them. And still for others, it is because sex was tragically used against them through abuse. All of these are rooted in the lack of a clear understanding of the sacredness of sex.

No matter how much knowledge you have about sexual technique, unless you embrace sex as a holy act, your sexual relationship will fall short of fulfilling the purposes for which God created it. On the other hand, discovering what God intended and combining those discoveries with skilled technique will set your marriage on a trajectory of which most couples can only dream.

SEX IN 3D

Do you realize that you are much more than just your physical body? Since the triune God created us in His image, we are made with a body, a soul and a spirit. He also designed sex to profoundly touch our entire being. Learning how to experience sex in all three dimensions will help you fulfill its purpose in your marriage and provide you both with maximum sexual satisfaction. We call this having sex in 3D.

Let's take a closer look at each part of our being and how it is involved during sex.

YOUR BODY (THE PHYSICAL DIMENSION)

Some people overly focus on one aspect of their being sexually and miss out on much of what God intended for them. The ascetics' influence on the early church's view of sex is an example of this from the past. Today, the obsessive focus on physical beauty and selfish gratification is an equally erroneous view that has fueled a culture of serial sex without commitment or emotional attachment – *"one-dimensional sex"* – at the expense of each person's soul and spirit.

Let's look at four significant aspects regarding the physical part of sex that are often overlooked.

1. Sex between a husband and wife is spoken of in Genesis 2:24 as their becoming "one flesh." In 1 Corinthians 6:16, the Bible speaks of this also taking place when an unmarried couple has sex. What is the significance of this becoming "one flesh"?

    Men and women were created by God to be His image bearers and to reflect His love for us. In Genesis 1:27, we read that the man and woman were created in the image of God; yet we know that men and woman are different physically and emotionally. When you, as a husband and a wife, engage sexually as "one flesh," together you more completely reflect the image of God and His desire to be united together with us in love.

2. Sex is very sacred to God, and it should be for us as well. Sex outside of marriage is a grievous offense. In addition to harming our fellowship with God, it is called a sin against a person's own body (1 Corinthians 6:18). Let's take a close look at that meaning. As Christians, our body is the dwelling place or temple of the Holy Spirit (1 Corinthians 6:19). Sexual sin forces the indwelling Holy Spirit to be a part of something against His will for us and is tantamount to rape. That's what makes lust, fornication and adultery so offensive to God and harmful for us.

3. God's amazing design of human sexuality on display as sexual intercourse produces an amazing physical experience. In addition to the following hormones mentioned that enhance emotional bonding, others like testosterone, norepinephrine and serotonin fuel sexual desire (also known as your libido), create physical arousal, and sustain ongoing sexual interest in

one's spouse. You see, God created your body to respond like this to encourage your monogamy.

4. Just as we are called to produce spiritual children of the faith by introducing others to faith in Christ, sex is designed to produce physical children. God calls children a "heritage from the Lord" (Psalm 127:3) and a blessing from Him.

   While procreation is an important part of marital love, it certainly isn't the only part. How do we know? Many portions of the Bible, including both the Old and the New Testaments, deal with marital passion, lovemaking and pleasure without any mention of procreation. Examples include Proverbs 5:19, Song of Songs 7:7-8 and 1 Corinthians 7:5. Sexual pleasure for a husband and a wife is God's idea and is for our pleasure, procreation, strengthening the marital bond *and* reflecting God's glory.

   From a practical sense, we can also see that sexual intimacy involves more than procreation alone. Consider married couples who want children but, because of infertility or other challenges, are unable to have them. There are also couples who marry later in life without intentions of having children. Who could possibly say that sex is less significant for couples in these situations?

Your Soul (The Emotional Dimension)

When a couple moves beyond the mere physical aspects of sex and truly connects emotionally, this *"two-dimensional sex"* takes on deeper meaning and personal significance. When you feel desired by your spouse, you feel special and loved. Sex provides that special opportunity for couples to connect. How does this happen?

When you experience sexual climax, a powerful cascade of hormones, including oxytocin and vasopressin, are released. God designed these hormones and others to cause you to emotionally bond with your spouse. Within marriage this is a wonderful blessing, and when you nurture this emotional connection and commitment, the depth of sexual pleasure and fulfillment also increases.

When sex is taken outside of marriage, the bonding also takes place, but now the repeated bonding and breaking of bonds has the opposite effect and becomes a painful experience for one's soul. Like the immunity one can develop to a drug, the bonding effect loses strength as it repeatedly adheres to someone and then gets torn apart. Each time the partners leave behind a piece of themselves, and the pain of another broken relationship causes them to put up protective walls to guard their wounded hearts. Rationally this makes sense, but relationally it has the harmful consequence of making it more difficult to bond to a future spouse.

What was designed by God to bond two people together so they could better withstand the stresses of life, no longer works as He intended. This is one of the reasons for our rising divorce rates and why couples who cohabitate tend to have lower levels of marital satisfaction than those who don't.[1]

You could settle for having two-dimensional sex, but that would still be settling for a counterfeit of what God intended. Some who get trapped in this limited mode find that they are never completely satisfied and often spend their lives bouncing from one relationship to another.

Your Spirit (The Spiritual Dimension)
The spiritual dimension of sex consists of two parts: the full blessing of God on your union and entering into your sexual relationship as a celebration of your marriage covenant and as an act of worship. Couples who discover this have the capability of experiencing sex at its fullest, or what we call *"sex in three dimensions."*

God's Blessing
Perhaps you have been trying to live your life without the peace, forgiveness and blessing of God, which can only be found in a personal relationship with Jesus Christ. We (Jeff & Glynis) didn't grow up in a Christian home and didn't fully understand God's plan for our lives until years after we got married. As a result, the early years of our marriage were very difficult, and we struggled to enjoy much beyond one-dimensional sex. It wasn't until we received Jesus Christ as Lord and Savior and yielded our lives and marriage fully to Him that we began to understand God's plan for us.

As we both grew deeper in our relationship with Jesus, we also grew closer to each other. As we experienced forgiveness for our sins and the unconditional love of Jesus in our lives, we were empowered by the Holy Spirit to more fully love each other in the same way. Prior to this transformation, we couldn't provide anything close to that for each other. We didn't know how, and our selfishness always got in the way.

God intended that *every* marriage would reveal new insights into His love for us. Just as oneness is displayed by the sexual union of a husband and wife in the covenant bond of marriage, you can become one with God through a new covenant by faith in Jesus Christ (1 Corinthians 6:19; John 15:4-5). If you would like to begin this journey, see Addendum 2. We are confident that you won't regret it!

We consider this relationship with God to be so pivotal in our marriage that I (Glynis) had Jeff's wedding ring inscribed with 1 John 4:19, which says,

"We love because He first loved us."

It is only after personally experiencing God's love through Jesus Christ that we have been able to have Christ-like love in our marriage over the past 35 years.

We (Julie and Randall) echo this rich significance of the Lord in our marriage. I (Julie) had "Ecclesiastes 4:9-12" inscribed in Randall's wedding ring. While the first verses in this reference describe how "two are better than one" because of the support they can provide to each other during difficult times, it is Ecclesiastes 4:12 that particularly resonates with us:

"Though one may be overpowered, two can defend themselves. A cord of three strands is not quickly broken."

A common interpretation of the word "three" in this context is that it is referring to the Lord as the third strand – that He is instrumental in strengthening our marital bond each day.

Celebration and Worship

We encourage you also to invite God to be present in the intimacy of your marriage. Just as communion is to be a regular part of a Christian's worship and remembrance of Christ's love and redemptive sacrifice for us (1 Corinthians 11:26), so should a Christian couple's remembrance and celebration of their marital covenant, expressed through sexual oneness, be a regular part of their worship. See 1 Corinthians 7:5.

In Ephesians 5, God reveals a fuller picture of the marital relationship when Paul declares that the marital cleaving – literally intercourse between a husband and wife – is intended to be a picture of the love of Christ for His church (Ephesians 5:32). God designed your marriage relationship to accurately represent His unbreakable covenant with His people. It is *only* within this context of security, exclusivity and the absence of any fear of rejection or abandonment that you can experience sexual intimacy to its fullest.

We agree with Tim Gardner who wrote in his book, *Sacred Sex*, *"The sacredness of sex is not based on how we treat it or mistreat it. Its sacredness is based on its essence, which comes from God. Sex is holy because God created it to be holy."*[2]

Going Deeper Together

1. What do you think of God's being the creator and designer of sex? Are you willing to entrust your sexuality to God? What difference can embracing this fact make in your marriage?

2. What areas – spiritual, emotional and physical – in your relationship do you feel are the strongest? What area would you like to focus on developing further?

CHAPTER 3

True Intimacy: Are You Having Sex, Making Love or Experiencing *Perfected* Lovemaking?

§

MANY TIMES, THE TERMS "MAKING love" and "having sex" are used interchangeably. That's unfortunate because there is a world of difference between them. In fact, couples who think making love is the ultimate love experience are still missing God's ultimate gift to married couples – an experience we call making *perfected* love.

Some people think the intensity of their orgasm will differentiate "sex" and "making love." An intense orgasm and the physical "connection" must mean the two people have "made love," rather than just have had "sex," is how the reasoning goes. But an intense physical response often masks the lack of emotional commitment. This reasoning is common in today's hook-up culture of casual sex. Participants may be quite adept at giving their partner a powerful orgasm, but the heart is neither deeply touched nor fully engaged in what is happening in those moments.

Perhaps sexual promiscuity comes from low self-esteem or low expectations of the other gender. For instance, a woman believing that none of the desirable men in her social circles are interested in a serious relationship may lead her to conclude that she needs to "give in," or she will be left behind. Such a compromise leads too often to simply having sex and trying to guard her heart from being hurt by staying emotionally numb to the situation or drowning the emotional pain with drugs or alcohol.

In the not-too-distant past, most people would have considered interactions like this as degrading and manipulative. Today, with so little value placed upon genuine commitment, casual sex has become the default mode for many single people.

> *"Every relationship we have, however brief and insignificant, influences every other relationship we have, and the patterns we repeat across relationships become very difficult to change."*

~ Dr. Dean Busby, director, School of Family Life

Sadly, the more people repeat this promiscuous pattern, the less likely it is they will recognize and build healthy relationships in the future.

Having Sex

From a purely physical perspective, most couples can figure out the basic mechanics of sex. It involves physical contact with another person's body that leads to sexual arousal and pleasure for either or both participants. Physiologically, sex *can* take place between two people with or without either of them having an emotional connection or commitment to the other.

In this physiological context, having sex is lust-based. The participants seek to fulfill their own selfish desires and once fulfilled, there may be little ongoing interest in the former "object of desire." For singles, the sex may be with someone who is okay being in a "friends-with-benefits" relationship. This attitude allows the non-committed person to easily move on if someone more desirable comes along or the level of excitement wanes. In this way, the person left behind has been objectified and controlled or manipulated as part of someone's selfish pursuits.

Even for couples who do start to form an emotional bond, this hyper-excited phase of love typically lasts between six months and two years. If a couple doesn't learn how to develop their relationship in other non-physical ways, they eventually lose interest in each other and move on. This is why we see so many serial relationship makers and breakers in our culture.

Many non-married couples have experienced so much pain in their love relationships that they resort only to having casual sex in an attempt to guard their hearts from the pain of being used. Unfortunately, this just leads to a hardened heart, where emotional responses are shut down, and sex becomes little more than the release of sexual tension and a self-centered, physical pleasure.

Singles don't have a monopoly on "just having sex." As married couples move past the honeymoon phase of their lives, it's not long before overloaded schedules, dirty diapers, ill parents and careers compete intensely for a husband or wife's time and energy. Sex may take place merely out of a sense of obligation, rather than a desire for deep intimate connection.

While there is nothing wrong with an occasional "quickie," if this practice becomes the norm, the marriage suffers. He gets into a pattern of ejaculating quickly, and she often foregoes orgasm. Over time, without the deep intimate connection and tenderness of emotional intimacy, the very act of sex becomes an undesirable drag (usually more so for one person), and then both suffer. As the quantity of sex decreases, the quality of the sexual experience tends to decrease as well.

In a marriage, negative patterns like this are rarely intentional. However, allowing such patterns to go unchecked can become the norm of how a couple interacts sexually. It stands to reason then that if you want healthier sexual intimacy to be your "standard," then you must intentionally walk in that direction.

MAKING LOVE

Making love requires a transformation from a focus on one's own pleasure to focusing on fully pleasing one's partner physically and emotionally. It's engaging emotionally and physically at a deeply intense level. Just like learning how to play a musical instrument, this takes time to develop to the point where you together can make sweet "music" sexually.

We don't deny that there are non-married couples in exclusive and, in some cases, long-term relationships where there is selfless sexual connection steeped in genuine emotional connection. Even so, this doesn't negate the truth that their sexual connection will never be what God envisions for them as a married couple.

And as for couples who are married, certainly many of these couples are "making love" and have let go of the self-centeredness that is so prevalent with casual sex. Could there be more for them beyond simply making love? We think so!

Perfected Love Making (PLM)

Perfected Love Making is much more than how a couple feels physically and emotionally when they have sex. This only takes place completely where oneness is found – and that's within the context of a God-ordained marriage. PLM is distinctly different (and better!) than having sex or making love because those experiences lack the oneness that can be found only when a husband and a wife are covenantally united before God in marriage.

God speaks of marriage in unique ways that separate it from all other relationships. When Christians get married, they are called to agree with God on His life-long covenant design. They confess any sin from past relationships and receive God's complete forgiveness (Philippians 4:7). They are fully committed to each other for life and to fulfilling God's purposes for their marriage. They stand there fully committed to honoring Christ, with no illusions of a back door or an escape hatch. No ultimatums or threats of divorce. It is the replacement of "you" and "me" with the unity of "us" as one.

As one, sexual pleasure is no longer something that we search for to satisfy ourselves; rather, it is an experience where we are one physically, emotionally and spiritually. It's what has been called "whole person communication." What you experience your spouse experiences also, and vice versa. You give yourself to your spouse completely and with abandon – just as he does for you. (See 1 Corinthians 7:4.) You welcome the Creator of marriage into your marriage and bedroom and follow His Word.

It is only in this covenant context that you have the assurance of God's looking upon your sexual intimacy with full approval and celebration.

PLM isn't about being perfect. It's about committing to and fostering total trust and security, without any fear of abandonment, harm or punishment. *"There is no fear in love. But perfect love drives out fear, because fear has to do with punishment…"* (1 John 4:18). This type of love requires each person to be fully known – emotionally, physically and spiritually – fully loved by their spouse and fully committed to honoring God through their marriage. Lovemaking like this doesn't happen in our own strength; it only happens as a work of the Holy Spirit in each of our lives.

There is also no fear of God's wrath because, as we have already said, perfected love involves obedience to God's Word. When you engage sexually only within your marriage, you are able to enjoy perfected love as God intended. That's why it is more accurate to describe this not as "lovemaking" but rather as "perfected lovemaking." Unfortunately, many couples make poor choices or have been hurt along the way, making it difficult for them ever to get to this point without the intervention of God in their lives.

So what have you been doing? Just having sex? Just making love? God has so much more in store for you!

> *"Do not conform to the pattern of this world, but be*
> *transformed by the renewing of your mind. Then*
> *you will be able to test and approve what God's*
> *will is – his good, pleasing and perfect will."*
>
> (Romans 12:2)

GOING DEEPER TOGETHER

1. If you had sex with other people or with each other before marriage, how did those encounters fall short of God's plan for sexual intimacy?
2. What steps do you still need to take in order to experience and enjoy Perfected Love Making in your marriage?

CHAPTER 4

Preparing for Your Honeymoon and Marriage[1]

WE COVERED A LOT OF ground in those first three chapters, didn't we? Now that you have a clearer picture of what God intends for your marriage relationship, let's take a close look at how to prepare for your honeymoon and the start of married life together. We are confident, though, that as you dig into this chapter, you will find specific tips and sexual insights that will be invaluable in the months and years ahead.

Look closely at your situation (engaged or married), and glean the aspects of this chapter that are relevant for your unique circumstances.

GETTING STARTED

Discussing sex can be challenging for many couples, especially for engaged couples. However, even as an engaged couple, do not completely avoid discussing sex. While you need to be wise about not stirring up temptation, you also need to recognize that healthy discussions about sex will be vital to your marriage. We thoroughly address this topic in Chapter 7.

As an engaged couple, rest assured that there are ways to ease past the potential awkwardness in these early conversations. One way is to look for indirect opportunities to discuss sex. When you see a news article or a blog post on sexuality or a sex-related topic, use this as a springboard for discussing each other's perspectives. In our sexualized society, you wouldn't have to look too hard for these "conversation starters."

Share your own opinions and ask for your partner's. Use "I" statements to share your thoughts rather than "You" statements to tell the other person how he or she "should" think or feel about something. Remember, this is the time for refining your conversation and active listening skills and to share in a mutually respectful way.

In order to verify understanding and validate each other's thoughts, ask clarifying questions and then paraphrase what you heard him or her say. If you have differences of opinion, discuss alternate ideas and look for ways to find common ground. Also, use these early discussions to compel you both to dig into God's Word together to genuinely understand what He says about sex.

Male and Female Differences

Once you have been married for even a short period of time, you realize that men and women display and experience their sexuality in different ways. The following chart provides a list of general tendencies of the differences regarding the sexual natures of men and women. These lists are not meant to tell you how you should behave; rather, they are general lists to help you understand from where each of you may be coming as you navigate sex in your marriage.

GENERAL DIFFERENCES IN HOW MEN AND WOMEN VIEW SEXUALITY AND SEX[2]

	Men	Women
Perspectives	* Physically oriented * Sex is one part of the relationship. * Physical closeness * Wants sexual variety * Sex is a high priority.	* Relationally oriented * Sex is integrated into the relationship. If the relationship isn't going well, sex is difficult. * Emotional closeness * Must have security and privacy * Other priorities in life can be higher.
Sources of Stimulation	* Visually oriented * Her body and scent * How she responds to him sexually	* Words, actions, emotions and touch * The condition of their relationship * Emotional connection is stimulating for her.

Primary Needs	• His wife's respecting and admiring him • His wife's desiring him sexually	• Her husband's helping her feel loved, cherished, and understood • Emotionally connected with her husband
Sexual Desire and Response	• Consistent desire • Easily excited sexually • Goal-oriented, focused on the pleasure and the orgasm • Orgasm is quick and intense. • Must have an orgasm to feel sexually satisfied	• Cyclical desire, based on her menstrual cycle • Excitement builds gradually • Easily distracted during sex • Orgasm is longer, deeper, and can be multiple • Satisfaction is sometimes possible without orgasm.

As a result of these differences, a wife often feels unloved when her emotional needs aren't being met by her husband. In the same way, a husband often feels ignored or disrespected when his physical needs aren't being met by his wife.

It is very common for couples to have different levels of sexual desire, especially during different stages of married life together. When this happens, couples need to seek to compromise, address any underlying issues that might be interfering with their sexual intimacy and serve one another in this area of their marriage.

Be careful. It is extremely destructive to a marriage for one partner to use sex as a means of manipulation by bartering for something else in return for sexual "favors" or by frequent denial for one's own convenience. Manipulation cheapens the gift of sex in your marriage and violates 1 Corinthians 7:5.

TIPS FOR YOUR WEDDING NIGHT

1. Try to be as rested as possible. If you are traveling a long distance to reach your honeymoon destination, then consider planning a shorter trip for the first night.
2. Relax as much as possible and anticipate cherishing each other. Take time to connect emotionally and spiritually. Verbally express your love and commitment to each other. Pray together.
3. Take time to refresh yourself. Shower, shave, brush your teeth, and use mouthwash. We (Julie and Randall) remember that it was important to us that, on our wedding night, we had a hotel room with a Jacuzzi tub. This gave us a great opportunity to take a bath together, relax in each other's arms, talk and connect before we had sex.
4. Bring along helpful supplies, such as bathrobes, a scented candle and matches, romantic music, personal lubricant, massage oil, etc. You could also have the hotel staff put flowers and champagne in the room or any other personal touches that would enhance the evening.
5. Nervousness can inhibit having an orgasm – especially for her. Discuss your expectations for the first night in advance (who will shower first or if you will shower/bathe together, how the room will be made ready, how you will greet each

other, what you each will or will not be wearing, praying together, and so on). Discussing your expectations can help you balance feelings of excitement and the anxiety you may be experiencing. You may consider undressing each other, as this can be a literal, symbolic and passionate expression of the reality that your bodies now belong to each other.

6. Let reasonableness, tenderness, and mutual understanding be your guide. You don't need to live up to any "standard" except what pleases you as a couple.

7. The emotional barrier of seeing each other naked is best broken during your first night together. If you feel nervous, rest assured that nakedness will become more comfortable. Do not try to hide your body from your spouse and do not keep the room completely dark; rather, welcome the opportunity to see each other naked. A nightstand table lamp or candlelight may make this more comfortable than the glare of an overhead light.

As a new husband on your wedding night, it is important to take things *slowly*. Take your time with foreplay and follow your wife's feedback regarding what she enjoys. If your initial sexual experiences are physically painful for your wife, slow down your thrusting and don't go so deep.

As a new wife, you may not be comfortable or relaxed enough or familiar enough with your body to have an orgasm the first time you have sex – or even the first several times. That's okay. It doesn't mean that sex won't be wonderful in your marriage. It will just take some time and practice as you get to know each other's bodies.

As a woman, if you are a virgin, you may also experience some pain with intercourse initially due to the rupture of your hymen.

You should gently let your husband know what you enjoy and what you would like done differently. Use this time to learn how your body responds to different types of stimulation. During this time, it is important for the husband to be understanding and to have a servant's heart without adding to any performance pressure or anxiety over her having or not having an orgasm.

As husband and wife in these early stages of sexual exploration, resist the urge to shut down when you feel anxious or unsure. Engaging in sex is natural, but mutual sexual satisfaction is a learned process. We are confident you will learn it if you embrace it as a learning process. As husband and wife, you need to progressively discover how to provide pleasure for each other. Don't be too hard on yourselves. Learning how to have an orgasm may take time, especially for her since it will be more technique dependent. Most women will not consistently experience orgasm through intercourse alone.[3]

DURING AND AFTER YOUR HONEYMOON

1. We suggest taking a shower together at least once during your honeymoon. Showering together can help you become more comfortable being naked in each other's presence. Developing this comfort level will be beneficial throughout your marriage, so the earlier you develop it, the better off you will be. Hopefully you will discover that showering together is not a special treat reserved for your honeymoon or vacation, but something that you occasionally can share throughout your life together.

2. Talking about what you like and dislike may feel awkward initially. Be understanding and vulnerable with each other,

and don't stop talking about how you are feeling – no matter how awkward it seems. Ultimately, you are each responsible for your own orgasm, in that you each must help your spouse understand what types of stimulation will bring you to climax.

3. Make sure your spouse knows what you like or dislike. Just be extremely gentle with each other so that egos and emotions are not hurt, and openness and vulnerability are not hindered. This mutual understanding takes maturity and a willingness not to become defensive.

4. If something awkward happens while you are making love, keep things light. Just laugh about it together and continue on.

5. Both of you should pay attention to the timing of the wife's menstrual cycle. Her sexual interest and response will vary over the course of the month. Make your wife's orgasm the top priority, especially during the first week or two after her period ends. Discuss how you will deal with sex if she has her period on her wedding day or during the honeymoon.

Christians often want to know what is "permitted" sexually in a marriage. We have devoted Chapter 8 to addressing in-depth many of the questions you may have. In general, though, keep your sexual intimacy exclusive, meaning it is only between you and your spouse, not to be experienced with any other person, real or imagined (no actual third parties, no pornography, no one watching you have sex, and no fantasizing about people other than your spouse).

Use love as your foundation. It is never loving to force a spouse to "perform" sexually. However, it also is not loving to be rigidly resistant to sexual play or sexual acts that are biblically acceptable in the exclusivity of godly marital intimacy. When one or both of you wrestle with questions about what is "permitted" sexually, embrace such questions as a vital opportunity to dig into God's Word, your own hearts and your marriage covenant to find the answers. God will not disappoint you in guiding you.

Developing Your Unique Couple Sexual Style

Can we let you in on some things that many couples miss? There are more ways to share and enjoy intimacy in addition to intercourse. Learning this early in your marriage will enrich your sexual relationship as well as provide additional ways to enjoy intimacy together in the years ahead. It comes down to developing your own style of intimately relating to each other. That will take some time.

Success in the bedroom is ultimately about increasing the "Big O" – oneness – in your marriage. This oneness is so important, yet many couples neglect to take this time adequately. In the Old Testament, a newly married husband was exempt from military service or official duties for a year in order to learn how to please his wife. You would be wise to take special note of that.

> *"If a man has recently married, he must not be*
> *sent to war or have any other duty laid on him.*
> *For one year he is to be free to stay at home and*
> *bring happiness to the wife he has married."*

(Deuteronomy 24:5)

Be creative and sensitive to each other's desires, preferences and comfort level. The following are some ideas to help you get started.

Fill your marriage with holding hands, hugging and prolonged kissing on a regular basis. Spend time kissing, cuddling and talking before going to sleep each night. Kissing is like a thermometer that shows the temperature of your relationship.

> *"Kissing is a means of getting two people so close that they can't see anything wrong with each other."*

~ RENE YASENEK

Give each other a backrub or massage periodically to relieve stress and to enhance emotional bonding. Doing this without genital touching will enable you to enjoy this physical closeness and pleasuring without the added pressure of sex.

Find ways to be sexually playful even when sex is not on the immediate horizon. For example, incorporate into your everyday interaction specific touches and words that have a shared hidden meaning understood only between the two of you. It can be the way you squeeze each other's hand or a certain touch or something you say that is not overtly sexual but has loads of sexual innuendo between just you two.

Periodically, enjoy a shower or bath together for some additional fun. This will probably include both genital and non-genital touch, and the mix can add additional excitement.

Raise the bar with more erotic pleasuring as a special treat. This could include manual stimulation, oral stimulation or the use of a vibrator, depending on your comfort level. These also can be incorporated in addition to intercourse, especially if you both haven't climaxed.

View yourselves as an "intimacy team," and be creative by both suggesting a new position to try. If you both like it, great! Add it to your repertoire. If not, try something else next time.

Conclude your lovemaking times with additional cuddling, kissing and affirming your love for each other. As you enjoy this time of "afterglow," pray together and thank God for the gift of love with which He has blessed you.

GOING DEEPER TOGETHER

1. After your honeymoon, discuss the ways that you would like your spouse to initiate sex.
2. What fuels anticipation and sexual desire for you?
3. Discuss:
    a. Why you each look forward to having sex
    b. Your feelings about nudity as a married couple and your body image
    c. How often you anticipate desiring sex
    d. Reasons that would be acceptable for declining a request for sex
    e. Your willingness to try new positions for having sex
4. Read a good Christian book on marriage and/or sex together each year. Alternate reading a few pages out loud to each other. You can find recommended resources on our website, http://pursuitofpassionbook.com.

CHAPTER 5

Turning on That Loving Feeling - Desire, Arousal & the Plateau Phase of Sex

§

WHEN IS SEXUAL DESIRE HIGHEST in a person's life and marriage? Plenty of stereotypes abound about this subject, but real life often contradicts those stereotypes. Certainly many young married couples have strong sexual desire. However, we also know of young couples where one or both of the spouses have low sexual desire, and the marriage is struggling because of it.

I (Julie) receive emails regularly from people in their 20s whose marriages lack the sexual desire that we so commonly associate with newlyweds.

And the stereotype that sexual desire goes by the wayside as a couple ages also doesn't always hold water. There are many examples of couples who discover (or rediscover) intense sexual passion in their 40s, 50s, 60s and beyond.

Suffice to say, sexual desire is something you can't take lightly. What's going on in your marriage sexually (good or bad) will more often than not have something to do with sexual desire.

What we can also tell you is that maintaining sexual desire over the course of a lifetime isn't always easy. In fact, lack of sexual desire is the number-one sex complaint of women, so continuing to learn what pleases each other and nurturing desire should be a key focal point for every couple.

Sexual Desire (Libido)

Sexual desire is rooted in the emotional, relational, physical and spiritual areas of our lives. What we do in each of these areas can both support and strengthen desire or undermine and destroy it.

There are several ways in which couples can enhance a desire for sex for themselves and each other. While what works for one couple may or may not work for another, consider what may be missing in your marriage and give the following desire builders a try.

Emotional & Relational Desire Builders

Emotional and relational intimacy is the process of deeply knowing your spouse and being deeply known by them. It develops as couples share their thoughts, feelings and experiences in an open and honest way. For this to happen, your marriage will need to grow to a point where both of you feel wholly accepted, respected and admired in the eyes of your mate – even when they know your faults, innermost struggles and failures. You also will need to develop a high level of trust in each other. Trust must be earned and that can come from being truthful, wise and reliable. Consistently being trustworthy will help defeat fear in your marriage.

"There is no fear in love. But perfect love drives out fear...."

(1 John 4:18a)

Be emotionally healthy. First, be sure to take care of your self-care needs. Reasonably taking time for yourself will recharge you emotionally and enable you to emotionally connect more when you are together. This is especially important when you have young children or an overloaded schedule. When you are worn out, you have nothing to offer your mate. It's all about balancing "me time" with "we time." If that's out of whack, your libido is likely to be as well.

Be friends. Friendship tends to be an underappreciated part of marriage; yet the positive impact of staying friends with your spouse is huge. Rediscover things that you enjoyed doing while dating. Shake your inhibitions, and rediscover your "inner child." Have fun together and be playful. Having your own private ways of having fun together will make your marriage relationship feel more personalized, both in and out of the bedroom.

Be safe. Couples need to provide a safe haven for each other. A key aspect of marital friendship is that you and your spouse have a shared sense of "having each other's back" and holding each other's deepest vulnerabilities in confidence. When you hear a husband say of his wife, "She is my best friend," his words speak authentically to the indescribable companionship and safety he feels with his wife.

Be sensuous. As a wife, give yourself permission to be sensuous. God has given you complete freedom to enjoy sex within your marriage. His Word tells us so. You don't have to fear enjoying sex too much or think that you have to stay away from sex because the world has polluted it. If anything, God wants you to celebrate it, including the uninhibited intensity and pleasure of it.

> *"For everything God created is good, and nothing is*
> *to be rejected, if it is received with thanksgiving for*
> *it is consecrated by the word of God and prayer."*

(1 TIMOTHY 4:4-5)

You can be both godly and sensuous with your spouse. Just as when God looked upon Solomon and his wife enjoying sex and said,

> *"Eat, O friends, and drink; drink your fill, O lovers."*

(SONG OF SONGS 5:1)

Celebrate. The Lord lovingly blesses you and your husband each time you celebrate your marriage covenant sexually as well. He sees everything, and He encourages you both to thoroughly enjoy His marriage gift. Don't hold back! It may sound strange to hear this, but when you and your husband have sex, it is one of the most tender and holy forms of worship.

Learn how to communicate about sex. Talking about sex may initially be difficult – especially if you are having challenges in other areas of your marriage, but pushing past that hurdle is vitally important.

Get comfortable referring to your genitals by their proper terms. (See Chapter 7.) Both of you knowing the names of your respective genitalia can be helpful when telling each other what you enjoy or don't like during sexual intimacy. While the use of nicknames for body parts can be harmless fun, the use of slang or crude language may indicate that you still need to grow more comfortable with your sexuality.

To make progress in this area, you will both need to be willing to be more transparent and honest in sharing your thoughts, feelings and desires. Handle these conversations very gently, guarding against being critical, judgmental or condemning in any way. Discuss what intimacy and romance means to each of you. Most likely, your views will be very different – and the amount of clothing involved may be also! But here's the key: neither of your views are wrong. You're just different, and understanding those differences can play a big role in keeping your sex life and marriage growing and interesting. In Chapter 7, we will focus more specifically on how to improve your communication about sex.

Stop nagging. Changing your spouse is God's job. Instead of trying to change your spouse's views (unless they have been impacted by porn, adultery or abuse), do something new from what each of you has learned about the other's needs and desires. If you feel challenged in this area, ask your partner for a list of things that would please him or her and put it in your wallet or purse as a reminder. Get over expecting your spouse to be a mind reader. Your spouse is not, and that's okay.

Don't compare or covet. It's easy to fall into the trap of comparison, especially when you look at someone else's marriage. You generally only see and hear about another person's good qualities, not the irritating ones that we all have and try to hide. God knows this, and that's why He tells us in Exodus 20:17 not to covet what anyone else has. A healthier and more constructive approach is to think of all the reasons to appreciate what you do have, instead of comparing your spouse to someone else or focusing on your spouse's faults.

Resolve past hurts. Are you holding onto a grudge or past disappointments? Forgiveness is a gift that you give yourself. It prevents bitterness from consuming you and destroying your marriage. Any unresolved or incompletely resolved conflict in your marriage eventually creates an emotional wall between you, and that wall blocks intimacy.

> *"Sexual health and satisfaction is directly influenced by the quality of relationship conflict resolution."*
>
> ~ MICHAEL METZ, PH.D.[1]

EMOTIONAL & RELATIONAL DESIRE DESTROYERS

Sexual desire begins in your mind. Your brain is your most important sex organ. What you allow yourself to think about sex, your spouse and your marriage really matters. The things that subdue or boost your libido are rooted in emotional, relational, physical and spiritual circumstances, experiences and perceptions, but these are all processed through your brain. If you have been harboring negative thoughts and feelings about your spouse or yourself, you may need to experience forgiveness and a God-directed renewal of your mind (Romans 12:2).

Some other areas for which you should be mindful:

Ignoring the past. Sexual wounds from past experiences also can be brought into a marriage and rob it of intimacy until the wounded person addresses these hurts, typically with the help of a professional counselor. Otherwise, you likely will repress your current sexual feelings or resist healthy sexual feelings in order to numb the pain from your past. We address this issue more in Chapters 12 and 13.

Neglecting your spouse. Building emotional intimacy takes both quality and quantity time. There just aren't any shortcuts in the process. Mutually satisfying sexual intimacy requires your both getting to know each other on a deep level and having personal time for rest and relaxation. For young couples just starting a career, beginning a family and establishing their home, finding this time can be challenging. Every couple's situation is unique, but we can tell you that you will need to find balance in your work and family time. Doing so may call for adjustments in your thinking regarding where you work, where you live and when you start having children.

Being rebuffed sexually will raise your frustration level and can kill desire. If you are the one with the lower need for sex, stretching in this area will be a wise investment in your marriage. The person with the higher need for sex may also need to temper his or her desire somewhat, so the two of you can happily meet in the middle. Otherwise, disappointments in the bedroom will eventually impact other areas of your marriage.

Depression. Clinical depression involves recurring low mood accompanied by low self-esteem and loss of interest or pleasure in normally enjoyable activities. Being depressed puts a damper on all aspects of your marital relationship. If you have five or more of the following symptoms for more than two weeks, seek proper treatment, which usually includes psychotherapy, medication or both.

* Feelings of sadness or irritability
* Loss of interest in sex and other activities you once enjoyed

- Changes of weight or appetite
- Changes in sleeping patterns
- Feelings of guilt, hopelessness or worthlessness
- Inability to concentrate, recall things, or make decisions
- Chronic fatigue or loss of energy
- Restlessness or decreased activity
- Thoughts of suicide or death

Note: If you have had a traumatic sexual experience that has left you feeling abused or ashamed, speak to a Christian counselor or a pastor, preferably one specifically trained in helping people heal from sexual trauma. God can release you from your past and provide freedom and forgiveness. Don't let your past define your future. It doesn't have to be that way.

Medications. If you are taking a medication that has sexual side effects that you are experiencing (See Chapter 8.), talk to your doctor to see if there are alternative options available or other ways of countering those effects.

Visual and Emotional Pornography. Keep your relationship clean and pure (Philippians 4:8). Pornography has *no* place in anyone's life. You never increase intimacy by bringing a real or virtual third party into your most intimate relationship. The use of porn is degrading to both the viewers and the people being viewed.

Did you know that porn excites the same regions of the brain that cocaine does? Pornography can be just as addictive as drugs. It's unloving, unreasonable and unrealistic to expect your spouse to behave like an airbrushed, surgically enhanced porn star. Those aren't real relationships being portrayed. Porn is a devious, slippery slope lead-ing to emotional and relational pain and the destruction of natural desire.

Other risks of which to be aware include seemingly innocent things that slowly pollute your mind and emotions – things that we refer to as *"emotional porn."* Romance novels that cross over moral boundaries or cause you to covet or daydream about being with a more romantic spouse, "reality" television shows that paint a false picture or true love by confusing it with lust, and conversations with friends that only trigger feelings of dissatisfaction and resentment are just a few examples of emotional porn that can cause you to lose perspective on healthy intimacy. None of these are beneficial to your marriage. Just as visual pornography creates impressions that no real woman can live up to, emotional pornography creates unrealistic romantic expectations that no real husband can achieve either. God created sexual love to be sacred – set apart for the exclusive enjoy-ment of a husband and wife.

In order to successfully break a porn habit, you will need ac-countability partners in your life. It's virtually impossible to break the porn habit alone. Additional resources are listed in Chapter 14, and you can learn more at http://pursuitofpassionbook.com.

PHYSICAL DESIRE BUILDERS

As a wife, your level of desire is closely related with how you feel phys-ically and relationally. If you are in good health, reasonably rested and your hormone levels are balanced, you are more likely to desire sex.

Serve each other. Wise husbands know, or have learned, that desire also "begins in the kitchen." By this we mean that a loving husband will look for ways to help out around the house or with routine responsibilities. With our twenty-first century hectic schedules, "choreplay" is becoming an increasingly important part of foreplay. Likewise, a wife should look for ways to help her husband when he is feeling overloaded or stressed.

What we have just described is sacrificial serving on the part of both a husband and a wife. But it's not the sacrificial serving alone that strengthens your marriage bond. What strengthens your bond is genuinely and humbly embracing the heart of the server. If one spouse is serving sacrificially, yet the other is consistently ignoring them or taking them for granted, this will become a source of resentment rather than endearment. Mark our words, resentment definitely will become an arousal killer.

Get physical. If you have fallen out of the habit of non-sexual hugging and kissing, reinvigorate your desire by remaking that a habit. Engage in prolonged cuddling and kissing on a daily basis. Touching releases the hormone oxytocin, which is commonly known as the "cuddle (or bonding) hormone." It's the same hormone that is released when a mother breastfeeds her baby, which nearly all women describe as an incredibly bonding experience.

Go to sleep at the same time as often as possible. And while you're at it, why not sleep naked once in a while? It may seem awkward initially, but you can learn to enjoy it. After all, you were born this way! You've gotten used to sleeping clothed, but you can learn new habits. In fact, if you don't have kids or roommates in the house, you might want to sleep naked all the time.

Be visually generous. Try to be more visually generous with each other and allow your physical desires to blossom. The one caveat we will add is that your husband likely is not going to care *what* you're wearing to bed – as long as whatever it is will be coming off on a regular basis! In other words, be intentional about initiating often and enjoying sex, and he'll be a lot more likely to look past that long flannel nightgown.

While we are talking about bedroom attire, husbands need to understand that wives typically are not as visually stimulated as men are. So while you as a husband may want to see your wife's body naked or in sensuous lingerie, your wife may want you to be *more* discreet in how you present yourself. If showing your naked body doesn't excite her very much, don't take offense. Consider investing in some nice boxers or pajama bottoms. Maybe the two of you could even choose them together.

Date each other. Remember when you first met and your relation-ship was exciting? Recapture that excitement. Schedule a date night that you know your spouse will enjoy and take care of all the details. You also can alternate taking responsibility for planning these dates. Plan ahead so it can be a time that you look forward to and pre-pare emotionally for lovemaking. Find ways to build in an element of delightful surprise for both your spouse and you to enjoy. If your schedule is on overload, this dating becomes more important.

Go away for an overnight escape. There is something special about getting away from the routine and household distractions. Even cou-ples without children living at home can benefit from an occasional night away in new surroundings and without distractions. If funds are tight, borrow a tent and camp out in the back yard, if possible.

Trade babysitting with another couple, and encourage them to invest in their marriage as well. Be creative. You can find a way to do this.

Serve each other sexually. Do something periodically for your spouse that you know he or she will like, but perhaps you aren't quite as fond of. Approach sex with an attitude of serving your mate, and your spouse will be more likely to return the favor sexually or in other ways.

For about 20 percent of women, physical arousal needs to be initiated *before* their desire for sex kicks in. This is the reverse of how men are wired. For a man, desire precedes arousal, so take careful note of that. Be open to engaging in foreplay – even when you aren't initially feeling fully "in the mood," and give physical touch a chance to trigger your desire for sexual intimacy.

PHYSICAL DESIRE DESTROYERS

Body image and beauty. How you view yourself physically has a great impact on your libido. Having a poor self-image produces inhibitions and shame and ultimately undermines sexual desire.

Sadly, only about two percent of women think that they are beautiful and less than 15 percent of women are very satisfied with their appearance[2] – even though the vast majority of husbands like how their wife looks. Most of us obsess over some tiny physical "flaw" involving our face, chest, rear end, hair, skin or nose, and we allow those perceived flaws to take over how we feel about ourselves.

When we hold ourselves up against the images that bombard us from media and magazines, it's no wonder we get discouraged. Actors and other celebrities all have at their disposal professional make-up artists, hairstylists, personal trainers, and wardrobe managers. Even the "everyday people" who appear as guests on talk shows first go through "hair and make-up" before appearing on set. In other words, many of the people we see on television, the Internet and in printed publications are rarely a reflection of what most people look like. Ironically, all those celebrities who look so stunning on the red carpet look strikingly similar to the rest of us when they are not professionally prepped for the cameras.

The body image war is waged on too many fronts to count, but ultimately only you can win it – and you can do it only by refusing to allow those fabricated images to take a toll on your self-esteem and your marriage.

We need a new definition of beauty and to stop allowing others to define what beauty is for us. There are only a few dozen super-models in the world. The other seven billion of us won't and don't need to look like them. Everyone's body is different, so learn to enjoy your unique beauty. Beauty is much more diverse than the current fads, and besides, God does a much better job at it anyway.

If we are so dissatisfied with ourselves physically, what does that say about our Creator? Do you really think He makes "junk?" If you need to eat healthy and exercise to shed a few pounds, go ahead and do it. You'll feel healthier and have more energy. Ultimately, how you view yourself will determine who you become, and you need to grow to a point where you can enjoy how you feel about your body rather than focusing on those negative thoughts that have been rambling around in your head.

Poor hygiene. Not practicing good hygiene before sleeping together is a major turnoff. Remember when you were dating and always wanted to look and smell your best? Don't let being married become an excuse for not being clean, shaved and smelling your best.

Flannel. Yes, you know what we're talking about – that heavy material that covers a woman from her neck to her ankles with very few access points! As a wife, invest in your bedtime wardrobe with some sexy lingerie, as well as some casual pajamas that are comfortable *and* sensual. Or better yet, husbands, why not buy your wife something a bit more sensual as a surprise?

Electronics. Occasionally turn off the television (and electronic devices) and talk together more. Do you know that on average, having a television set in your bedroom results in a 50-percent reduction in a couple's frequency of lovemaking? Is that sitcom, sporting event or reality show *really* worth it? Make your bedroom an "electronics-free zone," at least during the morning and evening hours.

Contraceptives. While some studies have shown conflicting results, hormonal contraceptives (such as the Pill, patch, DMPA injections, vaginal ring, etc.) may reduce some women's sex drive. While a multitude of factors impact a woman's sexual desire, it also tends to follow hormone levels during her normal menstrual cycle, peaking around the time of ovulation (about 14 days after her period begins).

Since hormonal birth control prevents ovulation, users experience less hormonal fluctuation and less sexual desire mid-cycle.

The key is identifying when your libido began being low. Did your libido drop around the time you began taking hormonal birth control? If so, discuss this matter with your doctor and consider a different method of contraception for three to six months to see if your libido returns.

On the other hand, if you have had times when your libido was high as well as times when it was low while you were using a hormonal contraceptive, you may need to examine your overall marriage relationship for an underlying cause. Possibly you need to build some additional margin in your schedule or address other factors that could be causing your diminished sex drive.

Spiritual Intimacy Strengtheners
Pray together. Do you know that the divorce rate among couples who pray together daily is less than one percent? Why is that so? Nothing brings a couple closer together than bearing your hearts before God and each other in prayer, and yet fewer than four percent of couples pray together on a daily basis.[3]

Praying together is both a solvent and a glue. It dissolves resentments and bitterness and binds hearts together. Per Swiss psychiatrist Dr. Paul Tournier,

> *"It is only when a husband and wife pray together before God that they find the secret of true harmony: that the difference in their*

temperaments, their ideas, and their tastes enriches their home instead of endangering it ... When each of the marriage partners seeks quietly before God to see his own faults, recognizes his sin, and asks the forgiveness of the other, marital problems are no more ... They learn to become absolutely honest with each other...."[4]

Spiritually connect. Imagine getting promoted at work and not sharing that news with your spouse. That's unimaginable. Now think about God's Word or a powerful sermon opening your eyes up to a new level of spiritual understanding or helping you break a bad habit. Wouldn't you want to share that with your spouse too? Sharing your spiritual life journey with those closest to you is a way of celebrating God's work in our lives. Doing this builds a spiritual intimacy that every marriage could benefit from on a regular basis.

Serve others together. People who generously help others tend to have a more positive outlook on life and relationships. Finding a way to minister together to others will provide you with a greater sense of purpose as a couple and keep the inevitable trials that you face in proper perspective.

Recognize the spiritual importance of sex. Think about it. When God was thinking of a way to tell His people how much He loved them, He could have chosen anything in the universe. Do you know what He chose? Marital love. When a couple comes together covenantally in marriage, that passionate connection of body, soul and spirit is the closest representation of God's love for His Church that is possible. God created marriage in order to communicate this truth about His love for mankind in a way that we could understand. Marital love gives us a language to better understand a profound spiritual truth (Ephesians 5:22-33).

> *"It's just as important to be filled with the Holy Spirit in bed as it is in witnessing to another about Jesus Christ."*
>
> ~ VONETTE BRIGHT, CO-FOUNDER OF CAMPUS CRUSADE FOR CHRIST

SPIRITUAL INTIMACY DESTROYERS

Carnality. Spiritual intimacy in marriage is undermined and can be destroyed when you live according to your fleshly desires (Galatians 5:13-21). Christians are called to walk in accordance with the leading of the Holy Spirit in their lives and producing the fruit of the Spirit. Read Ephesians 5:22-24.

Neglecting God and His Church. Our relationship with God only grows when we spend time with Him in worship, confession and prayer. If you neglect having time alone with God regularly, He will seem as distant as a stranger, and you will drift apart spiritually from your spouse as well. God has also provided a place for each of you to grow spiritually, to be accountable in your faith and to be encouraged. That place is a church that believes and teaches the Bible. We are told not to neglect meeting at church on a regular basis (Hebrews 10:25). When couples or individuals neglect this, their marriage (and children) suffers. This neglect sets a poor example for your family and exposes them to greater spiritual attack. Who ever thought church could be so important to your marriage and intimacy?

GOING DEEPER TOGETHER (PART I)

1. Read 1 Corinthians 13 together, and discuss each of the characteristics of love mentioned. How do you feel you are doing

in each of these areas? In what areas would you like to improve? Discuss how you can help each other grow.

2. On a scale of one (low) to ten (high), identify where you feel you are today regarding sexual desire. Discuss what factors or experiences have brought you to this place and what things you can try together to enhance sexual desire.

3. If sex always seems to end up at the end of your "To-Do" list, when could you schedule some time for extended lovemaking? Schedule a time when you are both likely to be as rested, relaxed and uninterrupted as possible.

4. Read Song of Songs together or read a Christian book on sex that will help you understand what God is saying to couples about sex and sexual pleasure. Ask the Lord to remove any fears or reservations that may be holding you back sexually.

5. What can you say to assure your spouse that you like his or her body as it is and are thrilled to be married?

6. Create a sensual feast for your spouse. For more on this subject, read Linda Dillow's and Lorraine Pintus' book, *Intimate Issues*, in which they provide a wonderful guide to having a "Gourmet Delight" dinner at home with your husband. This will be a night to remember for both of you.

7. What unresolved conflicts in your marriage still need to be addressed? If trust has been broken, apologize, make the necessary changes, be openly accountable and begin the process of rebuilding trust.

8. Share with each other the types of actions or things that communicate love to you and build emotional intimacy. Then make a list of three to five of those and begin practicing them for each other.

9. Have you been neglecting the spiritual aspect of intimacy in your marriage? Discuss ways that you can connect spiritually with God and each other and take the necessary steps to do so. See Addendum 2 for a guide.

Continue working on this for the long run. Building intimacy is a lot more like a marathon than a sprint.

THE AROUSAL PHASE

Each couple needs to discover their own sexual style, and that involves being vulnerable, transparent and adventurous together. Discovering what you like sexually and how you are aroused most fully happens best within the safety and security of a covenant marriage relationship.

Experience sex fully. When you have sex, take enough time to engage all of your senses. Focus on the sensations of touch, the sounds of romantic music, the smell of fragrance, and so forth. A "quickie" is fine once in a while, but if it becomes routine, you will miss so much of what your sexual relationship was designed by God to be. Spend enough time having sex for it to be a totally enfolding experience for both of you. Learn how to truly pleasure your spouse. Otherwise, if rapid-fire or one-sided sex is all you are experiencing, you will begin to associate sex with being unfulfilling, and it will become just another chore on your "To-Do" list.

Undress each other. Sometimes, it's not so much about what you are wearing but how you take it off. Turn on some romantic music and dance together as you undress each other. Continue dancing naked. Undressing each other can be a lot more fun than undressing yourself.

Stay focused. When making love, look deeply into each other's eyes. Speak to each other by name. This will help strengthen your association of sexual pleasure with your spouse. Focusing your attention where it belongs is especially important if you have had sex with anyone else in the past.

Find arousal triggers. Learn where your personal arousal triggers are located and how you like to be touched. This will take time, but it can be lots of fun to discover together. Ask your spouse to explore your body, or give each other a full body massage. Explore each other's body, and you will discover new erogenous zones[5] that you never knew were there, in addition to the obvious ones. These areas can provide physical pleasure when stroked, licked or sucked. Take your time and provide feedback regarding what feels good and what doesn't.

Incorporate total body touching in your foreplay. Help each other to tune out distractions and focus on the physical sensations of touch. In Song of Songs 2:6, Solomon laid beside his wife, placed his left arm under her head and fondled her body with his right hand. Place your hand on your spouse's and guide him or her to what pleasures you. Verbally sharing what you like will also heighten your experience with this mind-body interaction.

In response, we see Shulamith's being visually generous with Solomon in Chapters 4 and 5, as she reveals her body to him. He praises her for her beauty, beginning with her eyes and hair and working his way down to her breasts and genitals (metaphorically referred to as "fawns" and her "garden and mound of myrrh.") The arousal process is seen here to include both physical and verbal/emotional stimulation.

Learn to recognize arousal. When a woman becomes aroused, her heart rate and blood flow increase, causing her genitals and breasts to become engorged. This arousal results in heightened sensitivity to touch. Her vagina will also begin to become lubricated as her body begins to prepare for intercourse.

For a man, arousal causes his heart rate and blood flow to increase and his penis becomes erect. His scrotum begins to contract, lifting his testicles closer to the base of his penis.

Mix things up. What's your favorite food? Imagine having it every day for years. How excited would be you about that? Not so much. It's the same with sex. Keep things interesting by trying new positions, settings, massage creams and oils, fragrances, music, flavored body powder, and so forth. Even the missionary position can get boring if that's all you ever do.

The Plateau Phase

The plateau phase is actually a continuation and intensification of the arousal stage, leading up to the impending orgasm. For the wife, the outer portion of her vagina swells some more. During this time, sexual pleasure increases and remains at a heightened level, just short of the release of orgasm.

During this phase, the husband may secrete some fluid from his penis that can contain sperm, even prior to ejaculation. Couples should be aware that there is the potential for this to result in pregnancy. During this time, the head of his penis will enlarge and the penis may become firmer.

Going Deeper Together (Part 2)

1. Discuss what your level of desire for sex is currently like. What contributes to it? What detracts from it? How can you each be more understanding of any differences that may exist?
2. Make a list of fun things you enjoy doing together. Discuss how you can serve each other in this area of your marriage.
3. What comes first for you – arousal or desire? Is it the same for both or you or is it different?

CHAPTER 6

Orgasm - God's Gift for You and Your Marriage

§

"Sex has to be as good for her as it is for him if it is going to be good for both for a lifetime."

~ DR. CLIFFORD & JOYCE PENNER, SEX THERAPISTS AND EDUCATORS

FEW THINGS GENERATE AS MUCH excitement, confusion, thrill, frustration, euphoria, concern and obsession as orgasm. It's one of the most frequently pursued human experiences and yet, at times, can be one of the most elusive. Inability to orgasm during intercourse is the second most common sex complaint. It's easy to see how "lack of desire" and "inability to orgasm" can fuel each other in an unfortunate downward spiral.

Virtually every woman and man is capable of having an orgasm. God designed orgasm as a pleasurable experience for *both* of you. We encourage you to never stop looking through that lens. You are in this together, and you need to learn and master the techniques that will bring sexual satisfaction to your spouse.

In this chapter, we will discuss what an orgasm is, what is reasonable to expect, how to give and receive orgasmic pleasure and how to deal with some common challenges in this area of married life. We also extensively address orgasm in Chapter 7, where we cover the necessity of healthy communication about sexual intimacy. We are not being repetitive simply for the sake of being repetitive. We are trying to drive the point home that open communication plays a central role in helping each other experience pleasure.

What is an orgasm? In a clinical sense, defining an orgasm can be challenging. In fact, more than 25 definitions of orgasm are listed in the journal *Clinical Psychology Review!* For our purposes, we will describe an orgasm as:

"the intense physical and emotional sensation experienced at the peak of sexual excitation, usually resulting from stimulation of the sexual organs and/or erogenous zones and usually accompanied by pleasurable, rhythmic contractions in the pelvic area, muscle spasms in other parts of the body and ejaculation by the man."[1]

Her Orgasm

Your orgasm as a wife is one of the greatest determining factors in whether sex will be a treasured aspect of your marriage or a routine boring chore. Much in our culture overemphasizes a husband's sexual pleasure and underemphasizes a wife's sexual pleasure. The wise husband recognizes that both are important, and the more skilled you both become, the better your lovemaking will be.

Sadly, society has fed women a bunch of lies about her orgasm. Sex in the movies makes her pleasure look easy and instantaneous.

This inaccurate portrayal often creates false impressions and expectations regarding a woman's orgasm. Real women don't have an orgasm after 30 seconds of foreplay and thrusting or without any skillful lovemaking. Nothing is wrong with you if you can't orgasm on demand. You're not "abnormal." A woman's body just isn't made that way. God made your body differently than your husband's, so it stands to reason that you each will have to understand those unique attributes in order to experience optimal sexual pleasure.

Because it can be difficult for a woman to become comfortable with her sexuality and understand her body enough to orgasm, she can easily slip into a mode of thinking "It's just not worth it." The internal dialogue may go something like this: "I'll just make sure he has an orgasm. It's too much work for us both for me to climax. I don't want him to feel bad."

Before long, she may even rationalize that it is easier and better to fake an orgasm. It's no wonder that so many women resort to faking it because a woman's orgasm is much less visible than a man's. A wife may discover that her husband can't tell whether or not she is faking, so she resorts to faking as a means to an end. This approach is not a good idea.

A healthier pattern to build in your marriage is one where you both are intentionally seeking to help each other fully experience sexual pleasure.

Climaxing for a wife often is closely tied to how emotionally connected she feels to her husband. Virtually any healthy woman in a secure, loving marriage can climax when she has learned how to deeply experience the sensations of his sexual touch and her husband helps her relax while he applies what he has learned to do to bring her the most pleasure. Even if you have been married for quite some time and have not yet had an orgasm, don't give up. It's never too late to *learn* how to orgasm.

Obviously, having an orgasm is a process that involves your genitals, but to a great extent, what's going on in your mind and heart are more important. For a woman, orgasm is a much more holistic and complex endeavor, so keep in mind the importance of direct clitoral stimulation *and* staying mentally focused on the sensations of touch.

> *"Women are more likely than men to be distracted during coitus. If a woman hears a baby cry, recalls something that happened at the office, or wonders if she turned off the stove, her concentration can be interrupted. She has to reset her focus and rebuild her sexual excitement."*

~ HELEN FISHER, PH.D., ANTHROPOLOGIST

Think sexy thoughts during the day in anticipation of your time together and even more so while having sex. Flirt with each other during the day. Write a short love note and put it someplace he will see. Tell each other the things you are dreaming about doing later in the day.

Relax. If you are worried about having an orgasm or trying too hard, you are *less* likely to have one. Inhale deeply through your nose and exhale slowly through your mouth to release tension. Concentrate on the feelings of your husband's touch and tell him what you are feeling and enjoying. This will help you stay more focused on the sensations of touch and let yourself go completely.

There's a lot to be said for that saying "sexy is as sexy does." If you see yourself as a sensuous wife, you are more likely to appreciate your physical pleasure and experiencing it with your husband. Lose your inhibitions as you engage fully with this sensual experience. Actively express your passion and allow yourself to verbally express what you are feeling, freely. Hearing yourself verbally express pleasure will heighten your awareness of what you are feeling and provide feedback to your husband regarding what you are enjoying. Letting each other know when you are climaxing is a loving thing to do. If this is difficult for you, work on replacing any inhibiting thoughts that are preventing you from fully enjoying sex with your husband.

If you are concerned about your children hearing you have sex, consider putting on some soft background music in your room. Also remind yourself that even if your children do hear you, your sexual intimacy is nothing of which to be ashamed. Yes, you need discretion and privacy, but it's unrealistic and unhealthy to give children the impression that mom and dad never have private moments together.

Don't Let Modesty Rob You of Great Sex

As a Christian woman, you may find yourself wrestling with what it means to be "modest" *and* also be sexually uninhibited privately with your husband. Many of the Christian wives with whom I (Julie) speak find this to be a *huge* roadblock. They go to great lengths to dress and speak with modesty when in public, so that they will not compromise their Christian witness. It seems completely counter-intuitive for them to then switch gears and lose that inhibition when the bedroom door closes, and the lights go down.

If this is a struggle for you, recognize that being a Christian woman – particularly a Christian wife – is not one-dimensional. Yes, you honor God when you are modest in public, but you equally honor Him when you are sexually outgoing in the privacy of your marriage. Uninhibited sexual passion with your husband is holy and right and beautiful. God is as pleased with that as He is when you dress modestly when in public.

STIMULATING THE CLITORIS

Physical stimulation of your clitoris is necessary for you to have an orgasm. About 30 percent of women won't ever have an orgasm from intercourse alone – at least not from sex using the missionary position as it is commonly portrayed in movies. In the missionary position, a wife's orgasm will be more likely if her husband moves his body forward to a point where his erect penis is rubbing more directly on the clitoris. For most couples of average height, this may put his chest closer to her eye level.

Thrusting that is not at the right angle simply will not provide sufficient clitoral contact and stimulation due to the positioning of the clitoris relative to her vagina. The distance between a woman's clitoris and vagina can vary quite a bit, ranging from ¾ to 1½ inches (1.5-4.5 centimeters). If they are more than an inch (2.5 cm) apart, be sure to incorporate additional means of stimulation. In any case, don't fret. Over 90 percent of women don't always have an orgasm through intercourse alone. Having mutually satisfying sexual intimacy has a lot to do with your creativity and willingness to try different positions and forms of stimulation.

One way to provide sufficient stimulation to your clitoris during sex is for you to be on top, straddling your husband's hips. This provides you with more control over the positioning of your genitals and the rate of thrusting and more freedom of movement without having to be an acrobat. Placing a pillow below your husband's hips may also enhance contact with areas that you enjoy.

If your husband offers to pleasure you in ways that are new to you, trust that he does desire to please you in every way that he offers.

If you are one of the approximately 25 percent of women who have consistent trouble reaching orgasm, the use of a vibrator and/or manual stimulation, in addition to proper arousal and intercourse with your husband, can be a satisfying way to have more enjoyable sex.

Your husband didn't come with an inborn set of instructions on how to please you in bed. He may lack knowledge in this area or have learned inaccurate information from prior exposure to sex. Talk about your needs and desires. Remember that sexual technique cannot be compartmentalized. It's not about a rote list of steps to get from point A to point B. Great sex comes from a passionate blend of a wide variety of touches, positions, emotions, and expressions of pleasure. They meld into each other in a mysteriously delicious way that each couple is privileged to discover in their marriage.

TIPS FOR HUSBANDS

It most likely will take your wife longer to reach orgasm than it does for you. God made her that way, so learn to enjoy the journey as much as arriving at the destination. If you want phenomenal sex in your marriage, you simply cannot ignore your wife's pleasure.

*"Likewise, husbands, live with your wives
in an understanding way...."*

(1 PETER 3:7, ESV)

God calls you as a husband to be a student of your wife. This will take intentional effort on your part because she was created to be different than you. The following are a few things you should know in order to better understand how she responds sexually.

Don't stop romancing your wife. Help her to feel loved, confident and competent as your wife in her life as a woman and in the bedroom. Media often bombards her and undermines how she feels about herself, so she needs your encouragement and words of affirmation. Be there for her.

Connect emotionally. Don't forget to connect emotionally first. Since her brain is a key part of arousal, if you are concentrating only on erogenous zones, you're missing a key part of how she is aroused and desires sex.

Help her to relax and focus. According to brain imaging research, relaxation is the single most important factor in bringing your wife to orgasm. A great way to help her relax is to give her a massage; play her favorite, soft, relaxing music; pleasure her by candlelight; make sure that the children are occupied or sleeping; and the bedroom door is locked. Also ask your wife what she finds relaxing, as she may have suggestions that are not obvious. It's not about creating the perfect circumstances; rather, it's about treasuring your wife and making time alone as a couple a foundational attribute of your marriage.

Be patient. Including time for tender, arousing foreplay, it usually takes between 20 and 30 minutes for a woman to reach orgasm. Remember that true love is patient (1 Corinthians 13:4). Show your joy in watching your wife's sexual pleasure build. As you focus on helping her become aroused, you also will find that the wait will increase the intensity of *your* orgasm.

Provide proper stimulation. Use manual stimulation to bring her close to climax before penetration. Doing so may enable her to have an orgasm during intercourse.

Wet your fingers using either the secretions from her vagina, a lubricant or your own saliva. Initially, gently stroke her labia and the skin around her genitals. Ask her to guide you in what she is enjoying and the amount of pressure or intensity she desires. Begin by gently rubbing her labia and around her vagina. As she becomes aroused, use light touches and indirect stimulation around her clitoris to heighten the pleasurable feelings. You can alternate between using the palm of your hand and your fingertips, as different parts of your hand will vary the sensations. As your wife becomes more aroused, you may be able to apply slightly more pressure and direct clitoral stimulation. Follow her lead as to what she says she likes, even asking her gently, "Does this feel good?" She may find these verbal cues encouraging as she lets go of her inhibitions and embraces the pleasure.

Most people don't realize that the part of her clitoris that can be seen is only the tip. Her clitoris actually has two internal branches that extend behind her labia minora (inner lips) going down both sides of her vagina. You can stimulate this part of her clitoris by applying rhythmic pressure with two fingertips facing downward – like an inverted "V" – along both sides of her vaginal opening.

As you manually pleasure her genitals, you can also kiss her and stroke her with your free hand in areas that are sensitive and stimulating.

If she directs you on what to do or actually takes your hand or penis to guide it, don't take offense to this. As she becomes gripped by sexual arousal, it will be instinctual for her to do whatever she can to make sure the pleasure continues. Rejoice in her direction and her intensity.

Explore different angles of penetration to discover what she enjoys most. Some women enjoy having their G-spot[2] rubbed. This small, spongy area is located about two inches up the internal front wall of her vagina and swells during arousal.

Try massaging the area slowly with your fingers. The motion of your finger is the same motion you use when you indicate to someone you want them to come closer. Your wife may be surprised at how stimulating it is when you use your fingers to caress her vaginal area internally and externally. If she likes it, great. If not, try other things.

As your wife approaches orgasm, maintain a steady stroking rhythm around her clitoris with an amount of pressure that she enjoys. Don't change anything suddenly as this can break her concentration and make having her orgasm more difficult.

Also consider that at this point in her arousal may be when she most wants your penis inside her. There isn't a script to lovemaking.

It's not about a sequence of steps, but rather a journey where you both are growing in your awareness of each other's arousal and your own.

Her climax. While you may occasionally have simultaneous orgasms, your wife may appreciate it if you let her climax first – at least when she desires to have an orgasm. This will avoid potentially irritating her sensitive areas by thrusting and interfering with her response. It also gives you the opportunity to enjoy experiencing each other's orgasm.

Contrary to how your body works, you may find that your wife is able to have multiple orgasms. After her initial orgasm, she returns to the plateau stage when her body begins to relax. While a man's body needs time before having another orgasm, physically she doesn't. From the plateau stage, she can have additional orgasms within a short period of time, if she desires and you assist her. If you are wondering what it will take for her to have multiple orgasms, it has a lot more to do with her mindset than it does with your technique. Women are more likely to have multiple orgasms as they grow in their sexual confidence and embrace sexual pleasure as an experience worthy of pursuing fully. And if she does have multiple orgasms, they will likely come in quick succession, with subsequent orgasms possibly being stronger than the first.

Either way, don't get hung up on the number. That's not an indication of sexual prowess. Just take direction from her, as she may want gentler touch in those moments right after her initial orgasm – or she may want you to continue to thrust. It also can be helpful to her if you lovingly say to her, *"Tell me what you would like. Tell me what you need."*

His Orgasm

For most healthy men, having an orgasm is a fairly easy process. The continued stimulation of his penis, provided by thrusting during the plateau phase of intercourse, is usually sufficient to lead to an orgasm. If that is not the case for you, see Chapter 12 where we address common male sexual difficulties.

His orgasm will be intense but relatively brief and is typically accompanied by ejaculation. That said, most men enjoy additional stimulation of their genitals, which their wife can provide manually or orally, if you are both comfortable doing so.

Tips for Wives

One way in which your husband is different from you is that as sexual excitement and arousal builds, his body will reach a point of no return, seconds before ejaculation. While he is in the plateau phase, a time will come when it is impossible to stop the contraction in his pelvic area and the ejaculation of semen.

One way to increase pleasure for your husband is to allow him to see you fully experience orgasmic pleasure. This is a time to shed your inhibitions and self-consciousness and make some noise. He will greatly enjoy watching you experience orgasmic pleasure and feel validated as your husband as well.

His goal will always be to have an orgasm because that is how he is affirmed as a man, but you may desire to only enjoy the closeness at times. Letting him know what direction you would like to go will spare you both frustration. That being said, we recommend that your not having an orgasm be more of the exception than the rule.

Your being aroused is arousing to your husband, so if you downplay your orgasm too much, this will actually shortchange the sexual experience for both of you.

Want to really thrill your husband? Be spontaneous. Put the kids to bed early or arrange for them to sleep at a friend's house. Then tell him that you've been thinking about making love with him all day long. Then blow him away with a passionate time of lovemaking! Use your influence as a passionate, fully alive wife, and he'll be smiling for days.

Stimulating your husband should generally focus on specific areas such as the ridge around the head of his penis, the underside of his shaft and his testicles. Try different ways of providing stimulation, including varying rates and pressures in order to learn what is most satisfying.

Have you ever thanked God for how He designed you and your husband? Your differences can be a source of frustration if you let them get to you, or they can be faithfully embraced as a way to please and affirm each other for how you are different and how your differences can complement each other. God didn't make a mistake when He created men and women in His image. Accepting the way He created you can be your first step in finding peace in your marriage bedroom.

THE RESOLUTION PHASE

The orgasm phase is followed by a phase called *resolution*. During this time, your bodies return to their non-aroused state. This time can be important for couples to hold each other close and share loving thoughts while basking in the afterglow of their sexual experience. Take advantage of this time when you both have heightened oxytocin levels – the "cuddle hormone" – from just having engaged in enjoyable sex and enjoy this bonding opportunity to its fullest.

Staying connected increases desire and will set the stage for your next sexual experience. Some married couples find that right after sex is a great time to talk, whereas others like to drift off to sleep together. As a couple, be sensitive to what you each need in those moments. Through compassionate communication and discernment, you as a couple will settle into a healthy pattern of concluding your lovemaking.

Unless you have an urge to urinate, don't automatically rush off to the bathroom, which could leave your spouse feeling distant, taken advantage of and alone. Those aren't good feelings to associate with sex.

GOING DEEPER TOGETHER

1. After reading the previous chapters in this book, what are some new ideas that you can include in your lovemaking and marriage to banish boring sex?
2. Discuss the positions you each like most and why, as well as how often you each desire to have an orgasm.
3. Develop a playlist of relaxing and romantic love songs that you both enjoy to provide the ideal environment for lovemaking.
4. Buy cologne or perfume that you both like and use it primarily for romantic occasions. This can help you develop a stronger association between your spouse and sensual pleasure.

5. Discuss ways you can create an environment in your bedroom that is relaxing, romantic and stimulates your senses. Remove any clutter or distractions. Treat your bedroom as your special place.

6. Make "love coupons" that you can each redeem for special pleasures or favors whenever desired.

CHAPTER 7

Talking Together About Sex

*"We must not be ashamed to discuss what
God was not ashamed to create."*

~ Dr. Howard G. Hendricks, professor,
Dallas Theological Seminary

Married couples often want to know if there is a "secret" to amazing sexual intimacy. As you stand in line to buy your groceries, you could easily assume that the magazine publishers must know the secret. Oversimplified catchy headlines promise "Ten Easy Steps to Rock His World Tonight."

More than a few glances at advertising would have you believe that the secret is found in a pill or a potion. Televised commercials and emails claim to let you in on the secret – in exchange for purchasing the advertisers' products.

While we do not want to ignore the value of sexual technique or the positive impact of some legitimate, well-tested medications, we believe that a husband and a wife's experiencing enjoyable and mutually valued intimacy is the result of something much more foundational.

COMMUNICATION

Do you want to know the "secret" to amazing sexual intimacy?

Healthy, consistent communication about sex.

That's right. A husband and a wife genuinely and graciously communicating about their sexual intimacy is what leads to experiencing sex as God intended it.

We make it sound so simple, don't we?

We know from experience that good sexual communication in a marriage is *not* simple, but it is possible! With effort, practice and a shared commitment not to let differences or awkwardness become fortified roadblocks, you and your spouse can infuse your relationship with healthy communication about sex.

WHY IS COMMUNICATION ABOUT SEX SO DIFFICULT?

The reasons for this are as varied as there are married couples. Christians in particular may struggle because they have been told that sex is dirty, wrong or embarrassing. While the abstinence message definitely has value for people who are single, a common problem in Christian circles is that such a message is not balanced with a message that sex within marriage is good, holy and worthy of attention.

Sometimes communication is difficult because of past promiscuity, sexual abuse or other sexual transgressions. If someone has had negative or tragic experiences with sex, these events will likely hinder their ability to communicate about sex with a healthy outlook.

By its very nature, sex is an intensely personal and emotional experience. Whether someone enters into marriage having already had sex or as a virgin, that person does not generally speak openly and regularly about those experiences. We don't get a lot of practice talking authentically about sex, whether it is asking questions, being vulnerable about past sexual regrets, or expressing to a medical care provider symptoms or conditions involving our genitals.

It is indeed ironic that we live in such a sexually saturated society, yet a husband and wife often face huge communication challenges when talking about their sexual intimacy.

WHY IS HEALTHY COMMUNICATION ABOUT SEX SO IMPORTANT?

As with any aspect of marriage, sex has the potential for great conflict and pain, as well as profound connectedness. Books like this one, as well as other resources, can give you insights and tools to use. However, when all is said and done, the daily nurturing of intimacy in your marriage is your responsibility. A lot is at stake, so it is in your best interest to be humble and willing to learn how to communicate about sex.

In this chapter, we will specifically address how to discuss not only what you each like sexually but also any struggles or concerns you have about your sexual relationship.

Before we get to those specifics, the following are some general tips to consider as you begin this journey of healthy communication about sex:

1. *Recognize that the view each of you has about sex has been impacted by your own life experiences.* For example, what messages about sex did you receive when growing up (either direct messages from parents, the church, friends, etc., or indirect messages from media, entertainment and advertising)? If you had any sexual experiences before marriage, how have those impacted your view of sex? The more the two of you can talk about your different views and then seek to understand how they align or don't align with God's vision for sex, the better. You have to know where you're coming from if you want to get to where you want to be as a couple.

2. *Remember that when you entered into the covenant of marriage, you made an active decision that your marriage would be a high priority.* When it comes to communication about sex, don't lose sight of the fact that you are on the same team. Even when members of a sports team have conflicts, the ultimate goal doesn't change: succeeding as a team.

3. *Learn what safety means in communication.* Strive to listen without judging, keep conversations in confidence, and actively build vulnerability into your communication. By *vulnerability*, we mean "a willingness to be deeply transparent with each other about your fears, thoughts, confusion, joys, likes, dislikes, admirations, and love."

4. *Discern when circumstances are best for communicating about sex.* For example, if one or both of you is too tired, hungry or distracted, that's probably not the best time to have an intimate conversation about sex. Granted, you cannot let these factors

always be reasons to delay communication. You can, however, be intentional about creating space and time that are better suited for these conversations and setting yourselves up for success.

5. *Resist the urge to bring up struggles, especially serious struggles, when you are making love.* We aren't saying your bedroom can't be a good place to discuss your relationship, including your sexual relationship. Just be wise about when you initiate those conversations.

6. *Consider multiple forms of communication.* Yes, face-to-face communication is often ideal, but there is no reason why you also can't incorporate communicating other ways as well. For example, writing a letter to your spouse, with the goal of its being a springboard into verbal communication, can be a valuable way to communicate. Writing allows you to not only process your own thoughts, but also gives your spouse time to process theirs in response to what you wrote.

Typically, some husbands and some wives find it easier to discuss sensitive subjects when they are side-by-side, such as while taking a walk or working together on a project. If lying next to each other in bed seems to work for you, consider times that are not in close proximity to when you have made love or are going to make love.

Take the time to talk about the above suggestions so that you foster a shared commitment to make dialogue about sex a mutually valued aspect of your marriage.

> *"To be naked and completely unashamed means to stand before your mate and say, 'Here's my body.*

*Here are my emotions. Here are my thoughts about
God. Here is my history with all of my hopes, my
fears, my dreams, my failures. I stand here naked
– physically, emotionally, and spiritually."*[1]

~ Dr. Tim Alan Gardner, author of *Sacred Sex*

How to Talk About Your Sexual Intimacy Struggles

As you have likely already discovered in marriage, all struggles are not created equal. Whether the struggles have to do with finances, extended family, parenting situations, job demands, household responsibilities or a host of other issues, some struggles may be more consequential and harder to resolve than others.

The same is true of sexual struggles. It would be rare to find a married couple who has not encountered at least a few difficulties or miscommunications in their sexual intimacy. Some of those may be serious and deeply consequential, while others may simply be misunderstandings that are easily resolved. If you find your marriage in a place of sexual struggle, remember that you are not alone. Sex is a key aspect of marriage, so it is not unusual that something so vital to the fabric of your life together will occasionally be a source of discord.

Resist the urge to compare your journey as a couple with other couples' journeys. Certainly you can glean and learn from other resources, but your sexual intimacy as a couple is unique. It is yours to build, nurture, understand, protect and repair as needed. It is yours to own.

Here are some helpful tips as you communicate about sexual intimacy.

1. *Pray for your marriage and each other and for God's wisdom and direction.* When we approach discussions having first asked God to fill our hearts with love and compassion, we are much better equipped to look at struggles through His lens.

2. *Even if only one of you thinks there is a struggle, there is indeed a struggle.* There can be a tendency in marriage to chalk something up to "her problem" or "his problem," but that approach overlooks the one-flesh aspect of marriage. Yes, there will be times in your sexual intimacy when you both recognize something as a struggle, but don't be surprised if you also encounter times when one of you has more heightened concern about something. For the benefit of healthy sexual intimacy, don't ignore *any* struggle, regardless of who is bringing it up.

   For example, we often hear from people who are frustrated about their spouse's lack of interest in sexual intimacy to the point, in some cases, where the couple is rarely or never having sex. The spouse who is indifferent to nurtured intimacy tends to downplay or to dismiss altogether the frustration and pain this indifference is causing his or her spouse. Obviously, stonewalling isn't going to make the frustration and pain go away; it just intensifies it. We all want to be heard in our marriage, and that applies to the feelings we have about sex as well.

3. *Try to communicate about one struggle at a time.* While some struggles may be interconnected, if you try to address them all at once, the conversation will likely become overwhelming rather than productive.

For example, if a wife does not want to have sex because of her poor body image, two issues are going on. Her poor body image and the infrequency of sex in the marriage are the two issues. Instead of addressing both in the same conversation, consider focusing instead on the poor body image first. This can be an opportunity for a wife to genuinely share her concerns and hesitations about her body. A husband can help her not only explore the root of these difficulties but also receive his affirmations about her body.

Husbands, remind your wife often that God has crafted her body in a wonderful and beautiful way and let her know that she will always be your standard of beauty. Psalm 139:14 says,

> *"I praise you because I am fearfully*
> *and wonderfully made; your works are*
> *wonderful, I know that full well."*

This may sound crazy to wives, but most husbands find their wives to be "smoking hot" and think about them often. When he desires you sexually, he wants to make love with you. He's not as hung up on how childbearing and age may have affected your body because his desire is for you as the woman he loves. Some husbands even would say that it saddens and frustrates them when their wives are so hard on themselves and not comfortable with their natural beauty.

Likewise, as a wife, you too play a role in not letting poor body image take a toll on sexual intimacy. Your self-worth cannot be dependent solely on your husband's compliments, so strive to build a better viewpoint of yourself. If you want to get physically healthier, then do so. Using "poor body image" as an excuse to continually downplay or avoid sex is not a loving option.

4. *Don't expect the struggle to resolve itself.* Ignoring an issue or pretending it's not as serious as it is will not remedy the situation. If you want healthy sexual intimacy, you must intentionally move in that direction. That includes courageously and maturely talking about the struggles and being committed toward working together on solutions.

5. *Talk to each other respectfully.* Your spouse will be more willing to become more intimately engaged if you don't make your loved one feel inferior, incompetent or uncaring. Disrespect never changed or motivated anyone – at least not for the long haul. If your spouse approaches you about a concern, don't minimize your spouse's pain or get defensive. Genuinely listen to what your spouse is saying and sympathize with the emotions he or she is feeling.

6. *Ask for appropriate outside help, when necessary.* In many areas of life when we encounter difficulty, we seek someone who can help us. If you didn't know how to solve a problem with your car, furnace or hotel reservation, you wouldn't hesitate to ask for assistance, right? Why? Because the problem is frustrating you in some way. Sexual intimacy struggles are no different, so don't isolate yourselves or "wait for the problem to go away." Reach out to a professional Christian counselor or a mature marriage mentor for assistance.

Are you nervous about talking to someone else about something as personal as sex? Keep in mind that marriage counselors and mentors spend lots of time helping couples sort through an array of problems, so they have probably heard it all before and won't be surprised. Try to see them as allies rather than as people who will embarrass or judge you.

7. *Remember you are on the same team.* Even if you don't agree about a particular struggle, start with this agreement as a husband and wife: "We are committed to resolving together our struggles and not letting unhealthy patterns define our sexual intimacy."

8. *Strive for compromise.* As writers and speakers about marriage, we know that it is not unusual for some marital struggles to heighten to the point where each person's heels are dug in. Neither is willing to compromise, even if the struggle at hand is one where compromise is definitely possible. If you find yourselves stuck, look for ways to compromise and make your marriage less of a battlefield. If you are unable to defuse the situation, seek outside help.

How to Talk About What You Like Sexually

It's probably no surprise that talking about sexual struggles can be awkward and difficult, but what about discussing what you enjoy sexually? Do you find yourself stumbling through these conversations as well? For many couples, the answer is yes!

This hesitancy does not mean that something is wrong with your marriage. Talking about sexual pleasure, particularly your own, doesn't come naturally. Sexual pleasure is not a topic we get a lot of practice discussing as we are leading up to marriage. If anything, as Christians, we often spend a lot of time avoiding such discussions because of how easily they can lead to temptation.

Yet once you are married, being able to express what pleases you sexually is a skill worth developing. Understanding sexual pleasure – yours and your spouse's – is vital to the well-being of your marriage. In a sense, this is now part of your responsibility as a spouse – a sacred and rich responsibility that sadly too many couples downplay or overlook.

You may be wondering, *"But what if I don't even know what pleases me sexually?"*

Well, you're not alone! For women particularly, sexual pleasure can be complex. One main reason for this complexity is that the clitoris – the part of a woman's body where orgasmic pleasure is centralized – is not as predictable as the penis. That explanation may sound like a blunt way to put it, but many husbands and wives would agree with us.

GET FAMILIAR WITH EACH OTHER'S ANATOMY

In order to have satisfying sexual intimacy, it's important to have a basic understanding of the male and female genitals. We have included illustrations of the key organs involved in sex and reproduction, as well as explanations as to how the male and female genitals work together during sex.

THE MALE GENITALS

Let's start with the man's genitals, shown below in Figure 1.

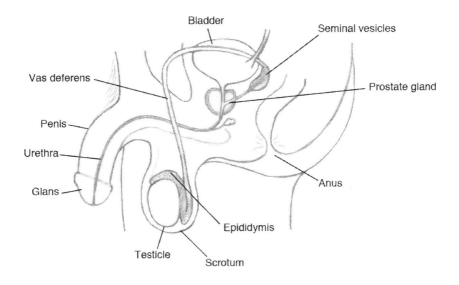

Figure 1 – The Male Genitals (Side View)

Glans – Also referred to as "the head of the penis," this area is highly sensitive to touch and stimulation. Figure 1 shows the glans exposed as a result of circumcision. For an uncircumcised male, a layer of skin known as the *foreskin* would surround the glans.

Testicles – Men have two testicles, made up of coiled tubes that produce sperm, which are located in the scrotum. As the sperm cells mature, they move to the epididymis, which is attached to the side of each testicle.

Epididymis – This structure is where immature sperm begin to develop their motility and ability to fertilize an egg.

Vas Deferens (Vas) – These are the two pathways through which sperm cells travel, by means of involuntary muscular contractions, to the seminal vesicles. When a vasectomy is performed, these tubes are cut and closed off after a section of the vas has been removed.

Seminal Vesicles – The vas deferens from each testicle leads to the seminal vesicles, which are located beside the prostate gland. Here mature sperm cells are stored and mixed with fluids that will be a part of semen. As the seminal vesicles fill up, a man feels a growing desire for sexual release.

Prostate Gland – Located just below the bladder, this gland produces a milky white fluid that makes up about two-thirds of the semen. This fluid, combined with sperm and seminal vesicular fluid, travels through the urethra in the penis and is expelled during ejaculation.

Later on, we'll explain in more detail how the male sex organs work together with a woman's body during sex.

THE FEMALE GENITALS

A woman's genitals are a slightly more complex, due to some of the areas critical for sexual arousal and orgasm being internal, and therefore, less obvious. Shown below are diagrams of the key internal (Figures 2a and 2b) and external (Figure 2c) areas involved during sex and reproduction.

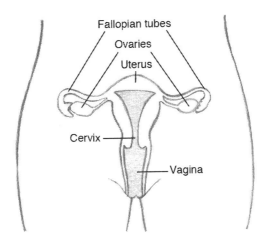

Figure 2a – Female Genitals (Internal – Front View)

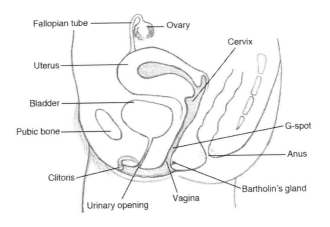

Figure 2b- Female Genitals (Internal – Side View)

Ovaries – Women have two ovaries, where *ovum* (eggs) are produced and released before entering the Fallopian tube. Typically, the ovaries will alternate releasing an egg each month. Usually this happens about 14 days after a woman's menstrual cycle has begun. When a woman is ovulating, her sex drive typically is at its strongest. The ovaries also secrete the sex hormones estrogen, progesterone and testosterone.

Fallopian Tubes – These are narrow tubes that lead from the ovaries into the uterus. Once an egg is released from the ovary, it travels through this passageway to the uterus, where it is either fertilized by a sperm cell or expelled from the body during her period.

Uterus – This organ is where a fertilized egg implants and develops into a baby. The Fallopian tubes are attached to one end of it. The other end of it leads to the cervix and vagina. If a woman does not become pregnant, she has a menstrual period whereby the lining of the uterus that had been built up to receive a fertilized egg is naturally "shed" through her menstrual cycle.

Cervix – The lower portion of the uterus that leads to the vagina.

Vagina – A passage of muscle and tissue that leads from the uterus to an external opening on the woman's body and secretes lubrication during arousal. This opening is called the *vulva*. The vagina receives the penis during sexual intercourse and also is the opening through which a baby is born.

Bartholin's Glands – Located within the vagina, these two glands secrete lubrication near the opening of the vagina.

G-Spot – A small spongy area located about two inches up on the internal front wall of the vagina. Some women claim that when this area is stimulated during sexual intimacy, particularly through manual stimulation, it produces a more intense orgasm.

Later on, we'll explain in more detail how they work together with a man's body during sex.

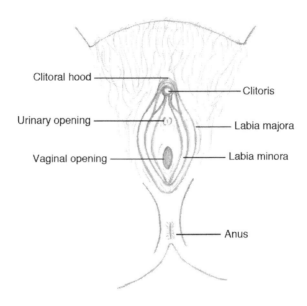

Figure 2c – Female Genitals (External)

Vulva – The *vulva* is "the external opening of a woman's vagina, including larger outer lips (labia majora) and smaller more internal lips (labia minora)."

Clitoris – A small organ above the vaginal opening, which includes a *glans* "head," as well as a hood. Its sole purpose is sexual pleasure in a woman and is extremely sensitive to touch.

It is not uncommon for newlywed couples to assume that having fabulous sex will just happen. More often than not, couples resting on this assumption find themselves sexually frustrated and confused. They keep waiting for the other person to instinctively know "what to do" in bed, only to discover that relying on mind reading or aimless trial and error is not the best path to phenomenal sexual pleasure.

It is also not uncommon for our pre-conceived notions about romance to hinder us more than help us. Women in particular tend to want sex to look like it does in their favorite romantic movie. Movies and television programs, though, are called make-believe for a reason. The directors and actors are depicting something to "make" you "believe" in something that is not truly authentic. Love scenes on the screen are carefully crafted portrayals made to look perfect by an off-screen crew of scriptwriters, lighting directors, make-up artists, hairstylists and props managers.

Long story short, when you and your spouse make love, no one will be there to fix your hair or tell you where to put the pillows. The good news is that real-life sex can be much better than depicted sex! You and your spouse have the opportunity to experience something far more authentic and profound.

SEXUAL PLEASURE

I (Julie) have a friend who is a doctor. She shared with me that when a married woman comes for a doctor visit, she always asks the woman about sex in her marriage and whether she is experiencing orgasm. Seems like a bold (and some would say, unnecessary question), right?

It's actually a vital question, and here's why: if a wife is not experiencing sexual pleasure, it is likely that she will have little or no interest in sex. Not only is she not experiencing the healthy benefits of sexual connection with her husband, she also is not experiencing orgasmic pleasure (which, by the way, has its own health benefits!).

In other words, it is in the best interest for you as a wife and for the strength and vitality of your marriage if you experience orgasm.

My doctor friend is quick to point out that occasionally she will have a wife respond to the question about experiencing orgasm with a hesitant, "Umm. I *think* so."

Orgasm is such an intense rush of pleasure, usually beginning at the clitoris and radiating outward, that there really is no doubt what you have experienced once you have had one. So if you as a wife are "wondering" if you have had an orgasm, you probably haven't yet experienced one.

Do not feel ashamed or embarrassed about this. As we said earlier, a wife's sexual pleasure can be complex, and reaching climax – the point of orgasm – is a learned technique. Together, a husband and wife can affect if a wife not only has an orgasm, but the intensity of orgasm as well.

Is orgasm everything, and does it have to happen every time? No. But as I (Julie) often say, "Orgasm is not everything, but it is a very important *something*."

A husband's orgasm is obviously important too, but it is usually not as difficult for him to climax as it can be for his wife. Some people have thought this is a cruel irony, but we as authors and sexual intimacy advocates actually believe God's design is ideal. God has given married couples a unique opportunity to truly learn about each other and lovingly serve one another. If orgasm universally came easily to both a husband and a wife, it is doubtful they would take the time to genuinely discover all there is to know about each other's bodies. Likewise, if orgasm was extremely difficult for both, we as married couples may give up too easily and quickly, thinking such sexual effort is not worth it.

While your spouse does play a role in helping you orgasm, most of the responsibility lies with you. What you understand about your own body and then are able to convey to your spouse will increase the likelihood that you will regularly climax during sexual intimacy. Getting that understanding is good for you, your spouse and your marriage.

We encourage you to read the below suggestions together. Not only will you learn about how to orgasm, but you will also learn how to have intensely satisfying lovemaking.

REMEMBER THAT YOUR INTIMACY IS A PRIVATE ENCOUNTER
In the privacy and exclusivity of your own sexual intimacy, you have freedom. Relax and do not become inhibited by thinking thoughts like, "What if my friends saw me in this position?" or "What if so-and-so knew we were doing this?" If you are extremely nervous and inhibited, you won't be able to relax. If you can't relax, your body will not want to respond sexually. In other

words, if you are not comfortable with the idea of having sex and enjoying it, you won't have an orgasm.

Pay Attention to Surroundings

We by no means are saying the setting has to be perfect because if you always wait for the ideal circumstances to have sex, you won't have sex very often. But we do think you'll enjoy sex more if the room is the right temperature, you are assured of privacy (keep a lock on your bedroom door and use it), and you feel relatively clean. A shower before sex can be nice and great foreplay if taken together. If there's no time for a shower but you are concerned about body odor, consider using a washcloth to freshen up or cologne or body powder. A lack of cleanliness can be a huge turn off for some people!

Appreciate and Nurture Foreplay

It is often said that women need more foreplay than men, but what we as authors have found in talking to many husbands and wives is that foreplay, especially extended foreplay, tends to make sex better for both of you.

Foreplay can include a variety of techniques, and through healthy communication, over time you as a couple will learn what you each like and don't like.

One common aspect of foreplay is caressing. Touching each other's bodies with varying degrees and types of touch can be soothing, relaxing and arousing – all at the same time. God has placed nerve endings all over our bodies, so explore every inch of your spouse's body. Pay close attention to using your fingertips and fingernails to create amazing sensations across the skin.

Some commonly forgotten areas that are arousing to touch can be the hair, head, ears, neck, inner thigh and lower back.

Another common aspect of foreplay is kissing. Some couples are surprised to discover that extended kissing, including passionate wet kissing, as well as kissing different areas of the body, can be incredibly arousing. Sadly, some married couples grow to see passionate kissing as unnecessary or "something they did when they were younger." Don't be one of those couples. Enjoy kissing one another – in and out of bed!

Get to Know Your Wife's Clitoris
As a wife, your clitoris is the main area of your sexual pleasure. If it is not adequately stimulated, you will not climax and possibly will be left feeling incredibly frustrated.

You likely will not know how much stimulation or type of stimulation your clitoris needs unless you at least a couple of times bring yourself to climax. We know that some Christians do not agree with us on this matter and believe masturbation is always wrong. We, however, think that if you as a wife have never climaxed, it would be helpful if you manually – with your fingertips – bring yourself to orgasm in an effort to better understand your body and sexual response.

This can also be a good exercise for you and your husband to do together, with his not only watching, but also participating through caressing and the use of his hands as well. For nearly half of women surveyed in a study conducted by Medical Information Service, this is how they experienced their initial orgasm.[2]

Locate your clitoris with your fingertips. You may need to use some lubricant or saliva so that your fingertips move easily over and around your vulva and clitoris. Relax and begin to explore, increasing the rate of your fingertip movement and varying pressure.

When you start to feel aroused or tingly in that area, do not be alarmed; rather continue to "lean into" the pleasure and mentally embrace it. You may be surprised to discover how hard and rapid the pressure needs to be on your clitoris for you to orgasm. You may want to use your husband's fingers as well, with your hand on top guiding the rhythm and pressure on the clitoris.

For the husband, exercises like this, as well as encouraging your wife to vocally express what is pleasurable, will help you better understand how your wife's body responds and contribute greatly to her experiencing orgasm during sexual intimacy.

Most women would describe orgasm as arousal that steadily builds to a peak, followed by waves of pleasure that pulsate through her body – beginning at her clitoris and radiating outward from there.

A common frustration we hear from wives (and some husbands) is that the wife is not able to reach orgasm through sexual penetration alone. We will be honest with you – sexual pleasure for a wife often requires positions other than the missionary position and often requires additional ways of stimulating the clitoris. This need in no way lessens or devalues the lovemaking experience. If anything, when a couple enjoys complete freedom in nurturing sexual pleasure, it usually intensifies their bond and love.

Sadly, some wives choose to fake orgasm instead of learning what it will take to have a real orgasm. Their reasons for faking can even seem noble, such as trying to bolster their husband's ego and assure him he is a fabulous lover.

We would encourage you as a wife, though, not to fake orgasm. Don't do it. Faking diminishes intimacy and introduces dishonesty into your marriage bed. Faking orgasm fuels doubt about your ability to have a real orgasm and misleads your husband regarding what provides you pleasure. Faking orgasm – and downplaying the value of your orgasm in general – will leave you feeling like sex is a chore. Trust us on this matter. We hear from countless couples where the wife is not interested at all in experiencing sexual pleasure. This total disinterest does nothing but cause distance and resentment. You will hurt your marriage if you do not see that your sexual pleasure is a tremendous opportunity to honor God and bond with the man you married.

Husbands, express to your wife that her pleasure is important to you and that you also want to discover what she finds arousing and orgasmic. Do not take offense if she must show you what type of stimulation she needs to have an orgasm.

As a man, you may, at some point in your earlier years, have heard or assumed that "real men just *know* how to please a woman sexually." Sadly, this attitude is what contributes in part to a wife's thinking she needs to fake orgasm.

As we have already stated, a woman's being able to climax can be wrought with complexities, none of which are reflections of her husband's "manhood." We are going to trust that you do indeed want her to experience sexual pleasure because you love her and want what is best for her. With that heart attitude, humble yourself and encourage her to show you and tell you what feels good. This honesty is vitally important for the health of your marriage and your sexual connection.

GET TO KNOW YOUR HUSBAND'S PENIS AND TESTICLES

Some people assume that because a husband, especially an inexperienced husband, rarely has difficulty climaxing, that there is little to actually learn about his orgasm.

Some wives, particularly new wives, think that all it takes for her husband to experience intense sexual pleasure is to have his penis within her. She is available and thinks "availability" readily equates to profound sexual encounter.

These viewpoints are shortsighted and tend to rob both the husband and the wife from experiencing sexual connection that really transforms and enriches their marriage.

As a wife, you will do your marriage a world of good if you take the time and effort to get to know your husband's penis and testicles. Do not see them as disgusting; rather, embrace them as God's design and a part of who your husband is.

While he will likely appreciate your touch on all parts of his body, the attention you pay to his genitals will play a key role in how sexually satisfied he is.

While they may not always say it in so many words, nearly every husband will admit that his wife's sexually desiring him is empowering to him as a man. That sexual desire makes him feel more masculine and equips him to tackle life's responsibilities. In other words, sex is never just about sex. It's about feeling incredibly connected emotionally, physically and spiritually to the woman he married. That sort of connection simply cannot be replicated in other ways.

Sexually desiring your husband means you have a positive attitude about sex, his genitals and sexual pleasure. As a wife, when you embrace this approach, you will likely discover that it can be arousing for you to arouse him.

Husband, don't assume your wife will know the type of touch and stimulation you like on your penis and the rest of your body as well. While we do encourage a healthy amount of exploration, we also think it is wise for you as a husband to lovingly tell her what you like. Some examples may include:

"I like it when you caress my testicles with your fingertips."

"I like when you firmly move your hand along the shaft of my penis."

"I like it when you put your hands on my inner thighs."

Wife, when your husband is guiding you and showing you what he enjoys, see this as an opportunity to honor him. The fact he has to show you in no way means that he doubts your ability to sexually please him. If anything, his being vulnerable with you about his sexual pleasure will strengthen the trust and sexual bond between the two of you.

We have no doubt that when the two of you fell in love and married, you did so with eager anticipation about building a life together. Part of building that life is having sex exclusively with each other. The sexual pleasure you each experience is sacred ground where no other person is welcome to participate. Embrace the opportunity to learn about your spouse sexually, and you will be amazed at the positive impact it has on that life you are building.

> *"When you get to know your husband's penis, you don't just honor your marriage. You honor God."*

> ~ Julie Sibert, IntimacyInMarriage.com

What if Sexual Pleasure Isn't That Important to Me?
This is something that some wives in particular will say. These wives tend to view sex as something for "him," and they "don't mind" rarely or never having an orgasm. Occasionally, it is the husband who has lost interest in sexual pleasure. He may still make himself sexually available to his wife, but rarely is he enthusiastic about such intimate connection.

On the surface, such approaches may look selfless and generous. After all, they are still "available" sexually – even though not fully engaged in the opportunity. We encourage you, however, to understand that minimizing the importance of pleasure actually is detrimental to your marriage.

Why?

There are a few reasons. First, God designed orgasm for both a husband and a wife to enjoy, and He wants a married couple to have sex regularly (1 Corinthians 7:5). The simple fact that it was God's idea should inspire married couples to pay close attention to its significance.

I (Julie) often tell wives that they should remember that the clitoris is the only organ in her body that serves no other purpose than sexual pleasure. It contains 6,000 to 8,000 nerve endings that connect to a network of nerves throughout the pelvic region. The specific arrangement of nerve endings varies slightly from one woman to another, so you and your husband will need to figure out exactly what provides the most pleasure when stimulated. God cares about a wife's sexual pleasure as much as a husband's sexual pleasure.

Second, when sex is void of orgasmic pleasure, it's no surprise that it becomes a chore for the person who is not experiencing pleasure. When we hear of wives "going through the motions" or treating sex like something to "just check off their to-do list," one of our first concerns is that the wife is not experiencing orgasm on a fairly regular basis.

A husband and a wife who have made sexual intimacy a vital and consistent aspect of their marriage understand what hinders or helps their intimacy. Both are even quite aware of her monthly menstrual cycle. Why? Because God designed a woman to want sex more when she is ovulating, which occurs typically about 14 days after the beginning of her period. (Hormonal birth control can weaken this naturally rhythmic rise in a woman's sex drive, so please read Chapter 5 for more information.) It is advantageous for a couple to make the most of these times of increased arousal. Wives who struggle with initiating sex on a regular basis would likely find it helpful to start initiating during this high arousal time as well.

If we simply stand back and consider the intricacies of God's design for sex, we will see that sexual arousal and desire are details to which He paid great attention for both a husband and a wife. When a husband and a wife place meaningful significance on the sexual pleasure they both are experiencing, sex becomes more enjoyable and a greater priority.

Third, bringing pleasure to your spouse is a remarkable privilege and joy. Husbands and wives who have great sexual intimacy clearly echo that sentiment. A husband finds it incredibly satisfying to see and feel his wife having an orgasm. Likewise, it is an overwhelmingly good feeling for a wife to know she is able to bring her husband intense sexual pleasure – and that she is the only one who is entrusted with such power and honor.

Fourth, orgasm is healthy for us! When a husband and a wife experience sexual climax, it not only bonds them and endears them to one another, it also is abundantly healthy for them. Sexual activity relieves stress and releases endorphins within the body that contribute to a positive sense of well-being. You can learn more about the health benefits of sex in Addendum 1. From a purely physical activity aspect, sex is obviously good for us as it is a great form of exercise that works our heart and our muscles. That said, you might not want to use it as an excuse to never go to the gym or to go for a jog!

God knew that sexual pleasure for a husband and wife would benefit them individually as well as together as a couple. If your lack of interest in sexual pleasure seems to have become a "norm" for you, explore possible causes. We cover many possible contributors to a lack of sexual desire in Chapter 8.

WHAT IS PERMITTED SEXUALLY?

When the topic of sexual pleasure is discussed, Christians often want to know what is "okay" or "acceptable" in God's eyes. We are confident that our next chapter will answer most, if not all, of your questions in this regard.

For now, below are some suggestions on specific aspects of sexual arousal and intimacy that should provide a foundation for your discussions together. It may feel awkward when you begin discussing what you like, but the more you push through this awkwardness, the easier it will become to talk about pleasure.

The key is to mutually value the freedom to express what you like and don't like. While the following sections give you good talking points, also recognize that sexual arousal rarely can be compartmentalized. Such matters as foreplay, touch, kissing and other expressions of sexual attraction intersect and overlap in a delightfully God-ordained way. Appreciating this overlap will help you embrace sexual affection as integral to the way you do life together. This is a much better perspective than seeing sex as nothing more than intercourse in your bed.

As Rick Johnson states in his book, *The Marriage of Your Dreams: A Woman's Guide to Understanding Her Man,*

> *"Tell your husband what you like or don't like in bed. Teach him where to place his hands and/or lips. Show him what feels good*

to you. Not only will you benefit but your husband will be much more fulfilled as a man. Trust me, he will not think less of you for your openness and honesty in this area. This might be initially embarrassing for some of you, but better a few moments of embarrassment than a lifetime of sexual frustration. You're also depriving your husband of the joy of knowing he's adequate to satisfy your needs when you don't help him to understand your body."[3]

FOREPLAY

In Chapter 5, we mentioned the importance of foreplay. We now want to address that subject in greater depth here because understanding what helps each get in the mood for sex plays a significant role in setting the sexual tone in your marriage.

The reality is that you may not know what arouses you until you try something. This is especially true as a newly married couple is learning about each other sexually, but it also can be true over the course of your marriage as desires and arousal triggers change.

One way to better understand and appreciate foreplay is to become increasingly comfortable with affectionate touch while you are clothed. Obviously if you are in public settings, your touch needs to be appropriate. But it is possible to convey physical – even sexual – interest in your spouse without being overtly sexual.

Holding hands is an obvious example, but you can also express affection by gently caressing your spouse's arm or placing your hand on the small of the back or around the waist. Foreplay in public settings can also include a certain way you look at each other or even certain spoken words that are subtle, yet full of a shared private meaning for the two of you.

Demonstrating physical affection in the privacy of your own home or in any other private setting are excellent opportunities for clothed foreplay. Do not be too quick to resist your spouse's expressions of desire for you. At the same time, be respectful of things that may be more of a turn off rather than a turn on. We (Julie and Glynis) often hear from wives who do not appreciate being heavily groped while standing in the kitchen making dinner. A light tender caress or a gentle kiss on her neck would likely be a better approach. (Of course, if your wife likes heavy groping, by all means…enjoy this connection!)

Foreplay in the moments leading up to sex can vary greatly. Generally though, a wife needs more foreplay than her husband, especially the younger the couple is. A husband in his 20s or 30s may be ready for intercourse before his wife is even fully unclothed.

If you do not learn to verbally express what you need, assumptions will be to your detriment. A wife may be thinking, "Can't he see that I'm not ready yet?!" while her husband is simultaneously thinking, "Can't she see how ready I am?!"

The truth is that there is a lot of pleasure in the process itself, so don't become too consumed with thinking that orgasm is the only event in town. A lot leads up to climax and after climax that is intensely bonding. Sadly, too many couples downplay or miss these moments.

Touch

How do you each like to be touched? Do you like gentle caresses or prefer firm embraces? Are there certain areas of your body that are more sensitive to touch than other areas?

One common mistake that both husbands and wives make is thinking that only certain areas of the body are centers of arousal. For example, a wife may think that the only touch her husband finds arousing is touch that is focused on his penis. As a wife, you may be surprised to discover how arousing your husband finds it to have you caress his back, massage his legs, gently stroke his testicles or run your fingernails along his arms.

A husband may think that the only areas his wife wants to be touched are her breasts and her vaginal area. But what if she also finds it pleasurable to have her feet massaged or her hair played with?

Do you see why communication about touch is so important? Give yourself the freedom to try different touches with each other and to express what you like and don't like. A statement can be as simple as "I like it when you run your fingers through my hair" or "It really turns me on when you caress my back with your fingers" or "I tense up when you squeeze my breasts too hard. Can you try being a little more gentle when you touch them?"

Experiment and explore each other's body and you are likely to find new areas where you find that kissing, massaging, licking, touching, or blowing on to be pleasurable. These areas might include the neck, ears, mouth, scalp, behind the knees or elbows, abdomen, thighs or lower back.

KISSING

Ahh, the kiss! Some married couples downplay the role of passionate kissing, but if you want nurtured sexual intimacy, kissing will likely play a key role.

Many of the same suggestions made regarding communication about touch apply to kissing as well. How do you like to be kissed? Where on your body do you like to be kissed?

Our mouth is full of nerve endings and possibilities for giving and receiving positive stimulation. It is no surprise that kissing and being kissed are closely associated with sexual arousal. You know that phrase "one thing led to another"? Well, the first "one thing" more often than not is a kiss. For this reason, dating and engaged couples striving for purity are wise to avoid prolonged kissing. If that's the case, then the flip side should tell us that married couples should welcome and embrace kissing, as it will nurture their sexual intimacy.

POSITIONS

The sexual position with which you are likely most familiar is what is often referred to as the missionary. Certainly this position does have its advantages. Humans are the only beings who engage sexually, face-to-face, which can enhance the closeness and tenderness of the experience. Also, it is likely one of the easiest positions for a couple to engage in.

However, there's nothing to say that this is the only position in which a married couple can have sex. In fact, some couples find other positions to be more, or equally, enjoyable at times.

For example, when a wife is on top, face-to-face with her husband, she may be able to better control the stimulation on her clitoris for increased pleasure. Also, if she is on top, she in a sense handles some of the physical exertion of sex, allowing her husband to be more on the receiving end of their lovemaking.

Another position to consider is a husband entering his wife's vagina from behind. It may take a few tries to figure out how you each need to be positioned for this to be pleasurable, but most couples who master this position and enjoy it find that it offers sensations that are different than those experienced with the missionary position.

Certainly there are other positions. You are limited only by your flexibility and imagination. Some couples particularly like sex on the couch or in a chair because there is support and leverage that often is not available in a bed.

If you try a position, only to discover it's more difficult than pleasurable, don't consider it a failure. Instead, learn to laugh with each other and give yourself credit for at least trying.

Ultimately, when it comes to positions, the two of you, through good communication, will likely arrive at two or three positions that are most satisfying in your sexual intimacy. Mix those up and keep things fun and exciting.

THRUSTING

During intercourse, the rate, depth and angle of thrusting will impact the degree of pleasure for you and your spouse. It's a common misconception that the deeper a husband thrusts, the more enjoyable this will be for his wife. If anything, thrusting that is too deep could actually be painful for a wife. That being said, thrusting that is too shallow may not be pleasurable for a husband. Communicating about your preferences is important.

Another factor that is closely tied to penetration is lubrication. When a woman is sexually aroused, the walls of her vagina and her Bartholin's glands secrete lubrication, making penetration more comfortable for both her and her husband.

Every woman's body is unique though, so whether or not the natural fluids her vagina secretes are enough can vary. Also, where she is in her menstrual cycle and her age affect her natural lubrication as well. When she is ovulating, her body is more easily aroused, and the amount of natural vaginal lubrication is usually greater. As a woman gets older, if she is breastfeeding, taking hormonal contraceptives or antihistamines or is diabetic, she is likely to need additional lubrication.

WHAT IF MY VAGINA DOESN'T FEEL WET ENOUGH, AND HIS THRUSTING IS PAINFUL FOR ME?
Artificial lubricants work quite well and can help ease the movement of the penis within the vagina. Artificial lubricants are usually made with water, oil, petroleum, silicone or a combination thereof.

Common lubricants found over-the-counter are such brands as K-Y Liquid®, Aqualube® or Astroglide®. You can also buy effective ones through the mail or Internet, including such brands as Sliquid® and Wet®. We are not recommending any particular brand; rather, we are simply making you aware that you have several options to consider. If you need more lubrication to make your sexual intimacy enjoyable, invest in your relationship and buy some lubricant.

Remember that if you are using a condom or diaphragm during sex, some artificial lubricants can break down the latex material. In general, water-based or silicone-based lubricants are better to use but never use oil-based lubricants, such as Vaseline or baby oil. If in doubt, read the lubricant, condom or diaphragm packaging, or talk to your doctor or pharmacist.

After menopause, the vaginal lining gets thinner and pain may result during intercourse. If this is the case, speak to your doctor about the possibility of using an estrogen cream.

TALKING
How verbal are you during sex? This question may seem odd, but some people find certain words or expressions of pleasure can further enhance the experience. Yes, it can be a big turn on for your spouse too!

Nothing is wrong with expressing your pleasure through words, moans and other audible sounds. Avoid using profanity or anything that would diminish the sacredness of sex or be offensive to your spouse.

If you are concerned that children or houseguests may hear your sexual expression, then you simply need to be discerning about how loud you can be. Another option is to have music playing in the background that will help cover the noise, verbal and otherwise, of your sexual intimacy.

AFTER SEX

Unless you have to urinate, don't rush to the bathroom immediately after sex. Have a small towel or two handy so you can easily dry yourself and then hold each other close to enjoy a time of afterglow. Verbally reaffirming your love and appreciation for each other can go a long way toward helping you both feel fully satisfied.

GOING DEEPER TOGETHER

1. If talking about sex is awkward for you, why do you think that is? Share with each other openly your answer to this question and pray about becoming more comfortable with each other.
2. If there are currently any struggles in your sexual intimacy, share these with your spouse (not necessarily to solve them right now, but to bring more awareness to each other about concerns you each may have).
3. Tell each other one thing your spouse currently does that you find arousing during foreplay. Do the same for something your spouse does during sex.
4. What is something your spouse doesn't currently do sexually that you think would be arousing (i.e., a particular type of touch, position, etc.)? Discuss how you can incorporate that aspect into your lovemaking.
5. Husbands, tell your wife why her having an orgasm is important to you.
6. Wives, if you have not yet had an orgasm or have difficulty having one, share with your husband your commitment to discovering how the two of you can make mutual pleasure more possible.

CHAPTER 8

Honest Answers to Real Questions About Sex

§

WE ALL HAVE QUESTIONS ABOUT sex, but sometimes we are afraid ask. We hear conflicting stories, values, experiences and suggestions. In the back of our minds we wonder, "What's okay and not okay? Does God have a position on the matter, or should I just do whatever seems right to me?"

Determining what is permissible sexually from a moral and biblical standpoint can feel challenging at times. We live in an age where sexual "freedom" is often translated into an "everything-goes" approach, and sexual pleasure at any cost is the standard.

HOW FAR IS TOO FAR?

We would like to address couples who are dating or engaged and then provide some guidance for married couples too.

As Christians, it's easy to feel "odd" when you aren't participating in what so many people consider "normal behavior." When your friends, even those who profess to be Christians, engage in sexual activity outside of marriage, you may feel alone in the battle for purity. You begin to question if chastity only limits your choices in partners, and you fear being left out.

While most people start with the question, "How far is too far?" that is like asking, "How close can we get to a dangerous fire without getting too badly burned?" Though it can be challenging to grasp this at the time, compromising physically always comes with a cost. God isn't trying to cheat you out of fun. In fact, when He calls each of us to live pure lives, He has our best interests in mind – physically, emotionally, relationally and spiritually.

Here is the bottom line. Before you get married, Satan will do everything he can to get you to be sexually active, against God's will. After you get married, Satan does everything he can to *keep you* from being sexually active, against God's will. True to character, Satan is saying, "Have a lot of sex before you are married! But when you are married, have as little sex as possible." Do you see Satan's manipulation – and how easily it snares? Satan is determined to harm you on both sides of your wedding day.

During our (Jeff and Glynis') work with couples for more than 25 years, we have seen many couples get so close to the flame that they suffered the consequences of being badly burned. We also have met couples who maintained their purity until their wedding day, and not one of those couples regretted their decision. Likewise, we haven't heard regrets from couples who were at one point having sex but then recommitted to purity until their marriage.

Observing these experiences has led us to challenge couples by asking what we believe is a wiser question: "How can you best glorify

God by honoring His design for sex and receive His grace and blessing in your dating relationship or future marriage?"

God calls us to hold our actions up to His Word in order to discern what is holy and pleasing to Him and ultimately most beneficial for us. We are called to live according to a higher standard.

> *"It is God's will that you should be sanctified: that you should avoid sexual immorality; that each of you should learn to control your own body in a way that is holy and honorable, not in passionate lust like the pagans, who do not know God."*

(I THESSALONIANS 4:3-5)

Sexual sin seems to be particularly debilitating. When you compromise in this area, your spiritual vitality always suffers, and that's a terrible place to be – especially when you are considering making such a significant life decision regarding future marriage.

BEING SEXUALLY PURE

Living on the edge of your moral boundaries is extremely difficult when you consider how easily passion can be stirred up. To stay sexually pure, couples need to set firm boundaries regarding the activities in which they engage, cultivate their spiritual walk with Christ, and build accountability into their lives.

Just like a champion athletic team, you need both a strong defense and a strong offense to win this battle. First, we recommend that couples identify the ways they will individually strengthen themselves spiritually, emotionally and physically. They might decide to join a small group Bible study, meet with a mature Christian accountability partner for prayer and encouragement each week, and get proper rest and nutrition.

Satan comes to steal and destroy that which God has reserved for us in marriage. Satan still uses this approach of casting doubt about what God said and seeks to get us to believe that his plans are better than God's plans for us. When a person develops his spiritual life in Christ through Bible study, prayer, worship and fellowship, he develops the strength necessary for defeating the enemy of our souls.

We also encourage couples to take defensive measures to protect themselves. This defense could include not watching movies that feature moral compromise, not being alone together for extended periods of time without a plan for staying busy doing something of value, limiting their time together when they are tired, not staying together in the same room when traveling overnight, and not intimately praying together.

Couples whom we have seen live victoriously over sexual sin have asked another person or couple to be their accountability partners and given them permission to ask probing questions about the purity of their dating relationship. A mature couple can serve both the role of accountability partners and mentors who help the couple develop the skills necessary for building a great marriage. All temptation finds its power when hidden from others. Accountability partners can rob temptation of its power.

We have developed a guide to help you build protective margins in your relationship that will help you find God's best in your lives, which can be found on our website under Download Resources. We consistently find that the engaged couples we mentor who take these measures become the best prepared for marriage.

> *"But among you there must not be even a hint of*
> *sexual immorality, or of any kind of impurity…*
> *for these are improper for God's holy people."*

(EPHESIANS 5:3)

Here are three good gauges to determine if your physical affection has gone too far or is at risk of going too far:

1. *Are you touching or rubbing up against each other in areas that would be covered by a one-piece bathing suit?*

   Interestingly, this same guide is often used when teaching children about "safe touch." In other words, in order to protect children from potential sexual abuse, we advise them that it is not okay for anyone to touch them where their swimsuit would cover them (the exception, of course, is a health care provider or safe adult legitimately helping the child with a medical or hygiene issue).

   The "swimsuit" guide is a good one for unmarried couples too. If you, as an unmarried couple, are allowing your hands or mouth to wander to such areas as the genitals, breasts and navel, then you've gone too far.

2. *Are you doing anything physically that you would not want other Christians to know you are doing, especially Christians close to you?*

   When I (Julie) speak to teens about abstinence, one of the boundary-setting tools I suggest is that they imagine any date they are on will be completely videotaped and then shown to their entire family.

If you conduct yourself as if other Christians were actually aware of your actions, then you are less likely to compromise your purity.

3. *Are you purposely putting yourself in situations where sexual arousal and temptation are easy?*

If you, as an unmarried couple, are consistently putting yourself in settings where you are assured of having extended privacy, you will be more likely to give into sexual temptation.

When two people are in love, the desire for sexual contact is often quite intense. This is as true for engaged couples as it is for married couples. Deep and profound love between a man and a woman is quite arousing. With that being the case, engaged couples obviously need to set boundaries that prevent sexual contact until they are married and can give themselves fully to that desire.

Consider what God's Word clearly says:

*"Watch and pray so that you will
not fall into temptation. The spirit is
willing, but the flesh is weak."*

(MATTHEW 26:41 AND MARK 14:38)

*"Flee from sexual immorality. All other sins a
person commits are outside the body, but whoever
sins sexually, sins against their own body."*

(1 CORINTHIANS 6:18)

*"No temptation has overtaken you except what
is common to mankind. And God is faithful;*

> *he will not let you be tempted beyond what you
> can bear. But when you are tempted, he will also
> provide a way out so that you can endure it."*

(1 CORINTHIANS 10:13)

Ask God to equip you in setting and maintaining boundaries of sexual integrity. Some people may think setting boundaries is completely unrealistic in today's world where sexual activity among singles is common, but we assure you it is possible and there are couples who do it, even couples where each person has had sex in previous relationships.

We (Julie and Randall) had each had sex with other people prior to meeting. For one, I (Julie) had been married previously, so obviously I had had sex. From the time Randall and I met until we were married, nearly two years passed. And yet we did not do anything sexual in that time. Was that easy? No. But was it possible? Yes! We are proof that two people can be deeply in love and resist sexual temptation until marriage.

"What if we have already gone too far? What now?"

First, we want to emphasize that shame is a tool of the enemy, whereas Holy Spirit conviction is a work of the Lord. There is a difference.

God doesn't want you to hide or retreat in shame and defeat; He wants you to seek Him, humbly ask for forgiveness and then repent. Repenting means you choose to walk in the opposite direction of sin.

*"In him we have redemption through his
blood, the forgiveness of sins, in accordance
with the riches of God's grace."*

(Ephesians 1:7)

If you and your fiancée are currently doing anything that is sexually arousing, then you need to ask for forgiveness and then choose to stop the sexual activity. Using the three gauges we listed earlier in this chapter is a good place to start as you establish new and better boundaries. Also, you may each want to have an accountability partner.

While there are always consequences of sexual sin – spiritual, relational, physical and emotional – God is willing to forgive if we confess our sin and repent from it. That's not a popular concept today, but it's a crucial part of restoration. Then God can begin the process of recovery and restoration of His design and plan for your lives.

One of our mentees adopted the term *"born-again virgin"* as she broke free from past sexual sin and took the steps necessary to walk purely with her fiancé. They both wrote out their commitment to purity, specifying what good things they would commit to doing in their lives (Philippians 4:8-9) as well as the unhealthy activities from which they would abstain. They shared their boundaries and accountability commitments with us, and we were able to check in with them each week, pray with them and encourage them toward purity. Our involvement provided them with the support they needed to walk in the freedom that comes when the chains of sexual sin are broken. We were also blessed as we met with them each week and saw the newfound joy and peace that they were experiencing in their relationship with God and each other.

Couples who have sinned sexually prior to their relationship or with each other also need to extend grace to each other, just as God through Christ has extended grace to each of us. Thankfully, we serve a God of second chances and when we confess our sins and are sincerely repentant, we can be forgiven through Christ (1 John 1:9).

"With divorce rates being so high, wouldn't it wise for us to live together before getting married to make sure we are compatible?"

Numerous studies have shown that couples who live together before marriage have a higher risk of divorce than couples who don't. While that may initially seem counterintuitive, cohabitation is actually practicing a low commitment relationship with an easy way out. That's hardly a test for compatibility or a commitment to a life together in marriage. Cohabitation doesn't allow for a couple to develop the critical contributors to future marital fulfillment, such as sexual purity, self-control, covenant commitment and delayed gratification. Without those, what are you really "testing?"

Couples would be much better off preparing to enter marriage God's way and with His full blessing.

"What if we live together and agree not to have sex?"

We applaud your desire not to have sex before you get married; however, there are still several good reasons why you will be better off not living together before your wedding.

1. *Cohabitation puts you in the direct path of temptation.* Let's face it, living together and sharing a bed is not the best way to fight temptation. Even if you are sleeping in separate bedrooms, you still have tremendous access to being alone with each other. If you are serious about saving all sexual activity for your marriage, the last thing you should do is move in with the person you love and to whom you are sexually attracted. *"Can a man scoop fire into his lap without his clothes being burned?"* (Proverbs 6:27)

2. *Cohabitation compromises your Christian testimony.* The Bible says to avoid even the *appearance* of evil (Ephesians 5:3; 1 Thessalonians 5:22). When two people in love are living together, the common assumption is that they are having sex. While they may not actually be having sex, the *assumption* still is a distraction when the couple is trying to reflect Christ-like behavior, particularly to those in their circle of influence.

   What kind of example will cohabitation set for your friends who are watching? How will those who do not know about your commitment to abstain sexually view your relationship with each other and with Jesus? The testimony of our lives affects how people view Christ, the church, and God's design for marriage. Many have rejected Christ because they don't see people who call themselves Christians boldly living out their faith. *"...I urge you to live a life worthy of the calling you have received"* (Ephesians 4:1b).

   Cohabitation presents a stumbling block to others who may be encouraged to follow in your footsteps without abstaining from sex.

*"...make up your mind not to put any stumbling
block or obstacle in the way of your brother or sister."*

(Romans 14:13b)

3. *Cohabitation trivializes marriage.* Living together detracts from
   the sacredness that God ordained for marriage alone. Living
   together prematurely adopts the social aspects and some of the
   relational aspects of marriage and, therefore, dishonors it. This
   practice goes against Hebrews 13:4, which says, *"Marriage
   should be honored by all, and the marriage bed kept pure...."*
4. *Cohabitation increases the risk of having difficulty with the transi-
   tion to marriage.* While abstaining sexually before marriage is
   always a wise choice, the limited difference in living arrangements between the day before and the day after your wedding
   can make it more difficult to suddenly "let go" sexually after
   abstaining during cohabitation.

Another factor to consider is what will happen if you decide to
break your engagement, which about one third of couples do. Your
heartache, finances, and even legal complications will be that much
greater because you have emotionally and physically bonded to a
greater extent than you would have if you hadn't lived together.

Every couple deserves to enter marriage with the full blessing of
God, and that comes from obedience to His Word. You can be assured that as you honor Christ in your relationship that, *"...the* LORD
*bestows favor and honor; no good thing does he withhold from those whose
walk is blameless."* (Psalm 84:11b).

"I wonder if my fiancée and I are sexually compatible. Shouldn't we have sex before we get married to make sure we are sexually compatible?"

Having sex before marriage is not necessary to determine sexual compatibility. Why would something sinful be beneficial for you? That kind of reasoning just doesn't make sense. Also, even couples who have had premarital sex discover that sexual compatibility within marriage is affected by a host of variables that just are not present before getting married.

We tend to associate the word "compatibility" with the word "instantaneous." We will just intuitively *know* immediately whether or not something clicks. That's not the case with sex. In fact, every couple should expect to be somewhat "incompatible" at first.

Once you are married, compatibility is an area where you will both need to work together to learn how to please one another and to be pleased yourself. If you work at it, you can become sexually compatible. God made you both that way. He equipped the two of you to fall in love and commit your life to each other. By His very nature, He doesn't then fail to equip you in your sexual connection and compatibility as husband and wife.

What would your criteria for "sexual compatibility" be anyway? Would your primary focus be more on yourself or your partner? Do you realize that everyone's sex drive changes over time with a man's sex drive decreasing somewhat during his 30s, 40s and 50s, while a woman's sex drive tends to increase during her 30s and 40s?

If you were to have sex before getting married to check compatibility, what would that experience tell you about:

- A lifetime of sexual compatibility vs. perceived compatibility at a single point in time?
- How much you will learn during your marriage about satisfying each other after years of intimate sharing and conversation?
- How each of your sex drives will change over the course of a lifetime marriage?
- What sexual fulfillment would look like in the midst of a secure, permanent, covenant marriage relationship?
- What effects illness, medical treatment, job stress, financial concerns and busy schedules may have on both of you?

Sexual fulfillment is found in a loving, caring and giving marriage where both partners commit to placing the needs of the other ahead of their own selfish desires. It's not found in focusing on some vague litmus test of "How good are you at satisfying my wants?" That focus just objectifies your partner.

A couple ultimately develops and deepens their sexual compatibility throughout a lifetime of sharing love, respect, trust and security in marriage. It's a journey during which two sinful, initially incompatible people learn to become one emotionally, spiritually and physically, through the work of the Holy Spirit in their lives and marriage.

"How much should I tell or not tell my fiancé about my sexual past?"

It is very reasonable to ask if your partner is a virgin, but you should also carefully consider if you would be better or worse off knowing the specific, minute details of past sexual encounters – especially prior to your partner's becoming a Christian. Consider if the details will lead you to a greater sense of closeness and security or stir up feelings of resentment and insecurity within you. Will the details provide fuel for future issues such as flashbacks, comparisons, or your imagination?

Many couples find that sharing every intimate detail does little to strengthen the marriage bond they are trying to form. In the end, only you can decide how to handle this discussion while keeping in mind what is best for your relationship.

That being said, we would encourage you:

1. Not to keep secrets from your future spouse. If you are not a virgin, you should be honest about it. Lying or waiting until you're married to tell the truth will only cause bigger problems with trust later on.
2. To get tested for any sexually-transmitted diseases (STDs) and sexually-transmitted infections (STIs) that you could potentially have and discuss the results with each other.
3. To discuss any past tragedy and trauma, including such experiences as abortions, rapes, or sexual abuse that you have experienced or been associated with. We strongly recommend professional Christian counseling if you have experienced any of these.

Our desire is that you would find true freedom from your past sexual history through Christ and with each other. Read Psalm 51 together to put any sexual sins in proper perspective. Determine if you can both see sexual sin as primarily being against God. Be sure that you aren't holding this sin against your partner while ignoring any other sexual sins of your own. Likewise, forgive yourself for that which God has already forgiven you. Don't continue to hold your own sexual sin against yourself.

Even with a demonstrated lifestyle change, including growth and commitment to following Christ, a person can be haunted by past sexual sins. Talk to your pastor or a mentor to help you determine how much of a hold this sin may still have in your life. Be sure that a sufficient period of time has elapsed to demonstrate that the grip of past experiences has been broken.

"One (or both) of us had sexual activity before we met and got engaged. I have two questions. 1) We feel guilty about our sexual past. What can we do as we prepare for marriage to get past this so it doesn't hurt our marriage? 2) Should we be tested for STDs/STIs before we get married?"

First, what have you learned from your past experiences and how do you want to change going forward?

Any time we deviate from God's design for our lives, we sin. That's not a popular word today, but it is real, and it's the starting place for addressing your past. Getting sin out in the open and confessing it to God and to those who have been hurt by it is necessary for healing to take place (James 5:16).

Realize that our God is a God of second chances. If we will confess our sin to God and *repent* ("turn from continuing that sin"), He will forgive us (1 John 1:9). Jesus has already paid for all of our sins and offers us the free gift of forgiveness (Romans 5:8-10). By God's grace you can now live beyond those past experiences.

Also, if you had sex in the past with others (or even with each other), resist believing the lie that you should just "keep having sex." God would not want you to continue to walk in sin. As we have already shared, repenting of past sexual sin and receiving God's forgiveness is one of the best steps you can take to help ensure such past doesn't wreak havoc in your marriage bed.

"What about STDs and STIs?"

While confession of sin and receiving God's gift of forgiveness through Christ deals with the spiritual and emotional issue, there may be a natural, physical consequence from our past that still needs to be addressed.

To answer your second question regarding STDs/STIs, getting tested would be a good idea. Then you will know if either one of you are at risk and if special precautions or treatments are necessary so you can enjoy the healthiest sex life possible when married. There are various types of STDs/STIs, and management and treatment of them varies as well.

Any sexual activity (not just intercourse) with an infected partner increases the risk of picking up an STD/STI. In many cases, there are no immediate, obvious signs of having an STD/STI. Having no symptoms doesn't mean someone is safe to have sex with. The safest way to know each other's STD/STI status is to get tested.

Condoms also don't protect couples from all STDs and STIs. Some STDs, such as genital herpes, can be spread by skin-to-skin contact with areas around the genitals that are not covered by a condom.

Every adult woman should have a regular Pap test and may need a test to identify any presence of high-risk types of the Human papillomavirus (HPV), which could lead to cervical cancer or throat and oral cancers if their spouse engages in oral sex. HPV is spread through any kind of genital contact (vaginal sex, oral sex, anal sex, or genital-on-genital touching). HPV is present in about 90 percent of sexually active people by age 25. Currently, no routine HPV test is available for men.

If one of you is infected, it is also a good idea for the initially uninfected partner to be tested every few years as a precaution.

TOPICS FOR MARRIED COUPLES

"What's okay sexually for a married couple?"

This is one of the more common questions we receive with regard to sex in marriage: *"What is okay and not okay sexually?"*

If you have asked yourself that question, you are not alone.

When a Christian husband and wife ask this question, it is usually because one or both of them want to try something sexually that they are not certain would be acceptable in God's eyes.

God gives couples a lot of freedom to explore and enjoy each other sexually within the exclusivity of their marriage.

God also knows that when it comes to sex, people can be their own worst enemies and fall into practices that are harmful to themselves and their spouse. In His wisdom and love, God has clearly instructed us about things we should avoid. Sexual practices that are expressly prohibited in the Bible include:

1. *Fornication* – Sex outside of marriage (1Corinthians 7:2; 1Thessalonians 4:3).
2. *Adultery* – Sex with a person other than your spouse (Leviticus 21:10).
3. *Homosexual Sex* – Sex between two people of the same gender (Leviticus 18:22; 20:13; Romans 1:27; 1 Corinthians 6:9).
4. *Prostitution* – Paying for sex (Leviticus 19:29; Deuteronomy 23:17; Proverbs 7:4-27).
5. *Incest* – Sex between closely related family members (Leviticus 18:7-18; 20:11-21).
6. *Rape* – Forcing someone to have sex against his or her will or without his or her consent (Deuteronomy 22:23-29).
7. *Bestiality* – Sex with animals (Leviticus 20:15, 16).
8. *Lustful thoughts or passion outside marriage* (Matthew 5:28).
9. *Use of Pornography* (Job 31:1).
10. *Obscene or crude language* (Ephesians 4:29).

Other sexual actions and aspects of sex are not directly addressed in the Bible. If you have doubts or are wondering whether something sexual is permissible, we suggest you as a couple prayerfully use the four scriptural principles listed below as a guide to seek the Lord's leading.

1. Is it prohibited in Scripture? If not, it *may* be permissible. (See 1 Corinthians 6:12a.)
2. Does it reduce intimacy and oneness or interfere with a healthy, enjoyable sexual relationship? If not, it *may* be permissible (1 Corinthians 6:12b).

3. Is this practice harmful, painful, dangerous or distasteful to either the husband or the wife? This includes emotional, physical or spiritual distress, or memories related to past abuse. If so, it's not permissible or beneficial (1 Corinthians 10:23). You will need to balance your "freedom" with your responsibility to love your spouse (Philippians 2:3).

4. Does it actually or potentially involve or include anyone other than your spouse or potentially expose either of you to others? If so, it's not permissible (Hebrews 13:4; Romans 14:13).

   Sexual intimacy needs to be exclusive between you and your spouse. By "exclusive," we mean that no other people are involved in your sexual intimacy: no one is actually having sex with you and/or your spouse, no one is watching the two of you have sex, you are not using any pornographic material, and you are not fantasizing about people other than your spouse.

If you are in harmony with each of the above four biblical principles, determine if God is giving you both a sense of peace about it. If so, go for it. If not, avoid it. See Romans 14:23.

God is full of wisdom (Daniel 2:20). He promises that He will give it to us if we ask Him (James 1:5). If you are considering trying a sexual practice that is not prohibited in Scripture and that meets the above guidelines, try it. If you both like it, consider it morally acceptable for you and enjoy a new way of providing pleasure and love for each other. If one of you feels uncomfortable or turned off, don't force the issue by manipulation or pressure. However, if at all possible, the hesitant spouse should seek to prayerfully fulfill what his or her partner requests, as long as it meets the four guidelines outlined above.

It's also important that you remember your sexual relationship is uniquely yours. Don't gauge what is right for your marriage by comparing your sexual intimacy to what others say is right for their marriage.

When you consider that God designed sex to bond and strengthen you as a couple, it's reasonable to see that He has given you great freedom in your sexual relationship with your spouse. Remember His words to Solomon and Shulamith:

"Eat, friends, drink, and be drunk with love!"

(SONG OF SONGS 5:1B, ESV)

"What if we have mismatched sex drives?"

Statisticians and economists have a saying that goes like this: "Anytime you compare two of anything, one will be greater than the other."

When you compare any two people, it's very likely that their sex drives *will* be different! So will their heights, weights, skill sets, intelligence levels, bank balances, heart rates, tolerance for change, and so forth. If any of these areas seem to be the same, try measuring them with a more accurate gauge and you will see the difference. That's because of natural variation and comparisons. Nearly every marriage has one spouse who has a higher sex drive – to one degree or another – than the other partner.

After all, what are the chances that you would meet someone who meets all the characteristics you desire in a mate and also has the exact same sex drive?

Suppose you desired sex twice a week, and your spouse preferred sex once a week. You would be the *higher* desire spouse. But now suppose your spouse desired sex daily. You would be the *lower* desire spouse – without changing at all. The reality is that neither person is right or wrong. People are just different.

Watch out for getting caught in a "pursuer-rejecter" cycle. Here the higher desire spouse continually pursues sex from the lower desire spouse who distances him/herself and by doing so, provokes his or her spouse to pursue harder or to look elsewhere. This cycle eventually fuels feelings of rejection, frustration and irritation that permeate the entire relationship, until the sexual desire is fulfilled.

When it comes to sexual compatibility, such character and personality traits as emotional maturity, developing a servant's heart, and being flexible will tell you more about your level of compatibility than your early sexual experiences ever could. Something is to be said about learning and serving each other as husband and wife. Also keep in mind that both of your interest levels in sex will change over time, with his typically moderating with age and hers increasing as she goes through her 30s and 40s.

When a person feels like he is starving, all he can think of is food. Sex is like that too. If you discuss your desires and the one with the lower desire is willing to be more accommodating, you will often find that after a while, the requests for sex from the more satisfied spouse will moderate to a level that is satisfying to you both.

Also strive to discern if the mismatch is a matter of time management and/or priorities. Your schedules often play a key role with your libido. If one of you is overloaded with responsibilities and commitments, is there a way you can help each other find better balance? Simple yet sacrificial changes may be all that's necessary to better balance your interest in sex.

As a couple develops their sexual technique so that they are both able to have orgasms fairly regularly, grows in their understanding of what sexually pleases each other and works on developing emotional and spiritual intimacy, they are likely to find that their interest in lovemaking meets at a mutually satisfying level.

"How can we keep our sex life fun and interesting?"

Below are 35 ways a married couple can keep sex fun. Just make sure that whatever you do meets the standards for sex as God intended and is enjoyable to both of you.

Tips for Husbands

1. Become a student of your wife's sexual likes and dislikes. While having an orgasm will typically be easy for you simply by thrusting during intercourse, God created your wife to become aroused more gradually through careful clitoral stimulation. This likely means you will need to stimulate her in ways that don't happen during intercourse. In the context of a secure marriage, your patient and skillful pleasuring of her will increase enjoyment for both of you.

2. Focus on her sexual pleasure and make that your priority, especially during the two weeks immediately after her period ends.

3. Take your time stimulating your wife during foreplay. Wait until her inner labia become enlarged before inserting your penis. This will take longer to occur than her becoming lubricated. Extended foreplay increases her desire and excitement.
4. Occasionally, take your wife away for an overnight "mini-vacation" at a nice hotel and bring candles, body lotion and romantic music. Take care of any childcare needs in advance.
5. Ask her if she would enjoy some new lingerie.

"If love is blind, why is lingerie so popular?"

~ AUTHOR UNKNOWN

TIPS FOR *WIVES*

1. Learn how your body works, especially your genitals, and kindly tell your husband what you like and dislike sexually. Once you learn not only how to have an orgasm but also to thoroughly enjoy it, you will be more likely to want to nurture sexual intimacy with your husband.
2. Initiate sex often and in creative ways. Your husband will greatly appreciate this and may respond by initiating in ways that meet your deepest relational needs. Many women find that desire increases after they are aroused rather than waiting for sexual desire first.
3. Don't fake an orgasm. Be honest with your husband and yourself and be intentional about valuing pleasure. You will both benefit by honestly working on "making sweet music" together.

4. Cater to your husband's desire for visual stimulation. Occasionally make love with at least some light in the room, such as a nightstand lamp or candlelight. Undress sensuously in front of him. Treat yourself to some lingerie that you both will find sexually appealing.

5. Ask your husband what he enjoys sexually and then seek to meet those desires.

TIPS FOR BOTH

1. Make your love life a priority in your marriage. If your schedule is overloaded, put time on your calendar for uninterrupted lovemaking. Be sure to schedule more than 20 minutes too!

2. If you suddenly find that you have some unexpected free time, don't fill it with another chore. Make love!

3. If you have a television in your bedroom, consider removing it and spend more time focusing on each other. Read a good book on marriage out loud to each other. Sexual intimacy in your marriage is likely to improve as you grow closer together.

4. You don't have to be a gymnast in the bedroom to change positions and try some new ones.

5. Have sex in a new location of the house...or outdoors. Just be sure that you are in a location that is safe, and you can maintain your privacy.

6. Go out on a date and let your husband know that you're not wearing underwear.

7. Add candlelight and soft, romantic music to your bedroom.

8. Give each other a full body massage with warm scented oil.

9. Do a chore for your spouse and say that you want to "save him or her some energy for later that evening."

10. Make a list of 5 to 10 new things you would like to try sexually with your spouse. What fantasies do you have for your love life together? Share your lists. Then each pick one and go for it. If it works out, great. If not, don't get too serious or down on yourself. Just laugh it off together (never at each other) and try something else on the list.

11. Increase the amount and types of foreplay, both before intercourse and throughout the day so that you warm up mentally and physically.

12. Learn how to strengthen your pubococcygeal (PC) muscle by doing Kegel exercises regularly. This involves flexing the muscle that you would flex when trying to stop urinating, midstream. Flex that muscle ten times and hold it tight for a few seconds each time. Repeat these two or three times each day. Most people find that doing that each day aids in the intensity, duration and frequency of orgasm. It also helps the husband's control as he approaches that point of no return.

13. Discover each other's "love language[2]" and speak that way more often.

14. Turn off the television, computer and cell phone and go to bed at the same time.

15. Read the Song of Songs together and try out some of the ways they sexually pleased each other.

16. Go to bed naked for a change. Pajamas and nightgowns can be both a physical and mental barrier to intimacy while skin contact releases oxytocin that produces relaxation and a better mood.

17. If you have been having sex infrequently, try Sensate Focus. (See Chapter 12.)

18. Stop smoking and get some exercise. Your physical health will improve and so will sex with your spouse.

19. Don't neglect the "little things" like saying "I love you."
20. Passionately kiss each other every day.
21. Take turns placing your hand over your spouse's hand and guiding him or her to pleasure you.
22. Develop innocent code words or touches that have a shared meaning for the two of you and clearly send the message, "I have plans for us later!" This can be a great way to express your sexual interest without resorting to overt gestures.
23. Undress each other as part of foreplay. Allowing your spouse to undress you can be a tender and vulnerable way to heighten sexual desire between the two of you.
24. Spend extended time caressing every part of each other's bodies with a variety of touches *before* actually touching the genitals during foreplay. This can heighten arousal.
25. Don't put it off. Life isn't a rehearsal. You won't get another chance to live today.

"Most of our friends use porn, and it doesn't seem to be causing any problems. What's the big deal?"

When it comes to determining what is healthy for your marriage, you should use God's standards rather than look to other couples or society. Pornography degrades the women and men who use it and are featured in it.

God clearly wants sex to be an exclusive encounter between you and your spouse. Pornography in any form shatters that exclusivity by inviting other people into your intimacy (even if the other people are really not there but show up in the form of images). Pornography usually involves explicit photos or videos of other people in sexually charged situations. For the purposes of defeating pornography in your life, we suggest that you consider pornography to be anything that triggers sexual thoughts or arousal that doesn't align with God's plan for you.

We strongly urge you not to bring porn into your marriage in any way, shape or form. Pornography use is a slippery slope that will do more to destroy intimacy than to strengthen it.

Also consider that your friends may simply be giving the impression that porn is not causing any problems in their marriage. More than likely, that's not the case; one or even both of them do have misgivings about the negative effects of such choices. And honestly, even if they don't have reservations, that doesn't change the fact that it is sinful and adulterous activity that deteriorates the covenant relationship between a husband and a wife.

"Is it reasonable for a husband and wife to expect to always have an orgasm during sex?"

Not necessarily. Having an orgasm is an intricate process, especially for a woman. Having sex is natural, but it takes a skilled husband and wife to bring her to climax. Much like how learning to play a musical instrument well takes time and practice, learning how to make pleasant "music" in bed also takes time, many loving discussions about likes and dislikes, experimentation with technique, and patience.

Developing mutually satisfying sexual intimacy takes a lot of understanding between you as husband and wife because having an orgasm is impacted by both of your minds, hormone levels, physical health, stress levels, spiritual state, distractions, safety, and mood fluctuations. Is it any wonder that having great sex can occasionally seem so elusive?

For most couples, there will be times when one spouse's desire is to only sexually please the other, particularly through oral or manual stimulation. While this is a nice complement in a couple's sexual repertoire, we encourage you not to allow this to become an ongoing substitute for the thrill of an orgasm through intercourse.

Good sexual intimacy will typically involve the wife's having an orgasm at least 75 percent of the time. A healthy husband should achieve climax nearly every time. The difference is primarily due to hormonal variations over the course of the month, the emotional complexity of the woman's sexual response and the fact that most of her sex organs are internal, making it a bit more difficult to access and observe the progression of her physical responses. Keep in mind, though, that for some couples, the wife's having an orgasm more often than that is her desire and expectation.

A husband should not assume that his wife will reach climax as easily as he does. Two thirds of women require additional stimulation beyond what takes place during intercourse. This is significantly related to the amount and types of foreplay in which you engage as well as the distance between her clitoris and vagina. The larger this distance is, the less likely the clitoris is to receive enough stimulation from intercourse alone.

Husband, if you had an orgasm as infrequently as your wife does, how would that impact your interest in sexual intimacy? Be a student of your wife and learn to please her as regularly as she desires. As we shared extensively earlier in the book, healthy communication about sex will increase the likelihood of you both consistently experiencing pleasure.

"What places are acceptable for a married couple to make love?"

While the bedroom is the most common location for sex, it certainly doesn't need to be the only place. Your main concerns should be privacy, comfort and safety. Some married couples find that sex in a different part of the house can be fun and offer variety. Couches and chairs lend themselves well to leverage and positioning that isn't always available in a standard bed. Again, just be sure no one is going to walk in on you.

In the Song of Songs, Shulamith suggests to her husband Solomon that they make love outside in the vineyard (Song of Songs 7:12). She and her husband were both the initiators and receivers of an exciting variety in their lovemaking. Married couples today should be just as creative, assertive and responsive.

While you may find it adventurous to have sex in a public or in a semi-public place where you can still maintain privacy, we recommend you err on the side of caution. For example, many workplaces have policies against any sexual activity on the premises, even if it would be taking place in a closed office or in the vehicle belonging to the person having sex. (If you own the company, you probably are good to go, but other than that, you'd be wise to not have sex at the office!)

Also, with the increased placement of security cameras in buildings, stores, restaurants, street corners, parking garages and so forth, some of the most "private" of public places are anything but private.

Be wise and make sure the exclusivity of your sexual bond is not compromised by other people's purposely or inadvertently viewing you having sex.

"Should I be concerned if I bleed after sex?"

If the blood is a light red color and this happens only once – especially after strong thrusting – it's probably just the result of irritation or friction. Try using a lubricant if low natural lubrication is a problem. If this bleeding happens repeatedly or if there's a fair amount of blood and/or pain, see your gynecologist. The blood could be coming from your cervix, your uterus or from an infection or other medical condition that requires medical attention.

"Is masturbation wrong?"

The Bible is silent on this subject so without explicit instruction from the Lord, we are left to apply general biblical principles. While there are strongly held differences of opinion among Christians, we believe the key issues to consider are your reason for masturbating, on whom your desire is focused and the impact of masturbation on your marriage.

Here are some thoughts for you to consider:

If you are unmarried, masturbation probably involves imagining another person or image being involved in the sex act. This would violate the teaching of Jesus regarding lust found in Matthew 5:27-28. Some would argue that a single man's masturbating could enhance his restraint in not fornicating, but that excuse would be covered under this passage as well. It's also important to note that the Lord has already made a natural and morally pure provision for the release of sexual tension through nocturnal emissions ("wet dreams").

One of the reasons God created our sex drives was as a motivation to marry. Seeking to satisfy our sexual desires through any other means destroys the motivation to marry and has contributed to the declining marriage rate today.

Being wise regarding the types of media one allows into his life also can minimize both the temptation and perceived "need" in this area. Many unmarried people make sexual purity more difficult by the choices and decisions they make in other areas of their lives.

For a married person, masturbation may be permissible under certain situations. If work, military commitments, travel or medical conditions prevent the couple from enjoying regular sexual relations, masturbation may be an acceptable substitute – either alone or together. Imagining one's spouse participating can help the couple remain emotionally connected when the physical connection is not possible. If there are times in your marriage when you will be separated due to circumstances like those previously listed, we encourage you to proactively discuss masturbation so you can together decide what is best for your marriage.

Some couples may find it arousing to occasionally include masturbation as part of their lovemaking.

We caution you to never completely substitute masturbation for sex. Also, do not use masturbation as a way to avoid addressing conflict or issues in your marriage. Masturbation during these situations would only serve to delay reconciliation in violation of Ephesians 4:26 and be detrimental to the marriage. Avoiding sexual relations when married also conflicts with 1 Corinthians 7:3-5.

Some believe that masturbation is never without sin because doing so would violate God's purpose of sex – bringing a husband and a wife closer together. We disagree that it is never without sin. When we look closely at Matthew 5:27-28, we find the reality that one person can bring another into an intimate connection as a result of the thoughts in his or her mind. When we apply this principle to a married couple, masturbating while focusing on your spouse, and in an effort to remain emotionally close when physically separated, can be a mutually beneficial experience.

Seek the Lord's leading on this matter. If you meet the prior criteria and the Lord gives you peace to proceed, fine. If He doesn't, the principle found in Romans 14:13-14 would indicate that you should abstain.

"Is it okay for us to use a vibrator or other sexual aids, such as sex toys?"

This question needs careful consideration as to the conditions of use, motives and potential consequences. A couple should first learn how to pleasure each other without the use of additional aids. Otherwise, vibrators or other sex toys may become a lazy substitute for developing the skill of naturally providing physical pleasure. See Chapter 6 for more information on how to please your spouse.

Some married couples, however, may find that using a vibrator or sexual aid adds variety and enhances their enjoyment when integrated into their overall sexual experience.

Our insights about masturbation would apply to sexual aids as well, such as a wife's using a vibrator during an extended absence from her husband. As a couple, you need to determine what is acceptable for your marriage in this regard. Even so, we encourage you not to use a sexual aid so frequently that you begin to associate sexual pleasure with the device – instead of with your spouse. God's design for your enjoyment of sexual intimacy with each other would be undermined.

In addition, using a sex toy as a means of avoiding having to deal with unresolved issues in your marriage is counterproductive and should not be done.

A few additional safety suggestions are in order.

1. If you purchase a vibrator or other device, be sure you are buying it from a company that doesn't sell, display or promote pornography. See Chapter 14 for additional resources.
2. There are no government or industry regulations regarding product safety testing, so be sure that quality, non-porous materials are used to reduce the likelihood of skin irritation, infection or injury. Silicone products are generally considered safe but are more expensive than those made from PVC or jelly-like materials. Products labeled as being made of silicone, but cheaply priced, are likely to be incorrectly labeled. Buy only from reputable manufactures, such as the Swedish company, LELO (lelo.com).
3. Avoid products that contain phthalates and those made of jelly, "sil-a-gel" or PVC, even though they are the cheapest and are used in the majority of products. Some studies have shown that these materials can cause a reaction with the delicate skin of the vulva, vagina and penis.

4. Any products intended for insertion into the anus are not recommended because using them increases the risk of infection and injury.

"As part of sexual play and foreplay, is it okay if we talk explicitly on the phone with each other (phone sex) or send sexy messages or images with our phones, computers or tablets (sexting)?"

In our technology-driven world, cell phones, computers and tablets (iPads, Kindles, etc.) are widely used to communicate with each other. These devices often have cameras and applications that make texting and creating photos and videos easy.

That said, you have to discern what is in the best interest of your marriage before you sexually connect with each other using these devices. Photos or videos that show you nude, semi-nude or in provocative poses could potentially compromise the exclusivity of your sexual relationship with your spouse.

Phones, computers and tablets are often borrowed or stolen. Don't assume that your security measures, such as passcodes, will prevent someone else from seeing these images. Many technically adept people can figure a way around those security measures.

You also have to consider the risk that you accidentally send the message to someone other than your spouse. Who among us hasn't mistakenly replied to one person via texting when we really meant to reply to someone else? It happens all the time, and the potential for it to happen when you are excited about sending a sexy text or photo is high.

What about racy texts that don't include images? Yes, it can be fun to use "innocent" words that are not overtly sexual or that have a shared meaning between the two of you. Just don't give detailed descriptions that you really would not want anyone else reading.

As for phone or video sex, where you are having a "live" conversation that is not being recorded, you as a couple may find this to be a fun and arousing way to stay connected. Just be wise to ensure no one can overhear your conversation.

One last point – if your employer issued you your phone, computer or tablet, then technically the company owns those devices and/or owns the service on the devices. In other words, do not use your company-issued device (or even your own device on company time) to send sexy texts and images to your spouse or have phone sex. Some companies have the capabilities to monitor what happens on their devices. Misusing the devices could be embarrassing for you and your spouse, not to mention grounds for discipline action and/or termination.

"What about privately taking videos of our lovemaking that we can then view later?"

We are not supportive of this idea because of the risk that someone else at some time may see the video. If the video is stored digitally on a computer, phone, camera or external hard drive, over time you may forget that the material is actually there. Years may pass and the day may come when your teenager is using your old computer, only to stumble across sexually explicit videos of you. If that thought doesn't cause you enough trepidation, consider that computers and cameras are regularly stolen or lost.

Lastly, while it may sound like fun to videotape you and your spouse making love to view later, our bet is you wouldn't find it very arousing. If you think your video will look like sex in the movies, you'll be disappointed. When a production crew choreographs sex scenes, they go to great lengths to make sure nothing looks awkward or messy. Real sex, on the other hand, *is* awkward and messy! Real sex, of course, is better than fabricated sex – but you may rob yourself of some of that delight if you view it on a screen.

"Often my spouse seems to never get enough sex. We just don't seem to be on the same wavelength. Any suggestions?"

Good communication is a critical part of every healthy, happy marriage. You can't expect your spouse to be a mind reader, especially when it comes to sex. Discuss both of your interest levels regarding frequency and how you will communicate your interest in having sex. While having this discussion may seem obvious, many couples fail to establish this practice and both people are left wondering if their spouse is satisfied sexually.

The husband who seems to always be in the mood may not be longing for sex as often as it might appear. His responding to your availability sexually may be in response to the offer being made. Having sex at that time may not have even been on his mind. So talk about your true intentions, desires and how you can communicate your desires clearly. Look for balance. If either one of you place too much or too little importance on sex, the level of intimacy in your marriage will suffer.

"What is the 'normal frequency' for a married couple to have sex?"

"Normal frequency" for any couple is primarily based on whether they are both satisfied with the level of intimacy in their marriage. If you are both satisfied and sexual desires are not being satisfied individually (i.e., through masturbation) or through any immoral means, then you shouldn't be overly concerned with how your frequency compares to another couple's.

The one note, though, that we would add to this answer is the rare instance where sex is rarely or never happening in a marriage, and both people are "satisfied" with such low or non-existent frequency. This situation is a red flag for us. If there is no reasonable justification for the lack of sexual intimacy (injury, illness, separation due to military or job commitments), then a married couple should be having sex or at least some form of sexual connection on a somewhat regular basis.

If one or both people are unsatisfied with the frequency of sexual intimacy, they need to compromise to find a level with which they can both live. Couples who have been married for at least two years often find that a frequency of sex somewhere between two or three times per week and two or three times per month to be satisfying. A married couple who has sex less than ten times per year is generally considered to have a "sexless marriage."

To make a long story short, we can't definitively answer this "frequency" question for you. The two of you will need to pay close attention to your sexual intimacy to learn what frequency is healthy for your marriage.

We will tell you this – struggles about frequency are some of the most common sexual struggles in a marriage. If you find that this area has been or is becoming a struggle, then you need to talk about it and strive toward finding a satisfying solution.

One of the most discouraging emails I (Julie) received was from a husband who wrote these words in describing the lack of sex in his marriage: "I vowed monogamy when I got married, and she gave me celibacy."

It's helpful and wise to ask yourself regularly if you are rewarding and blessing your spouse's commitment to you in marriage or are you making him or her regret it?

When a couple works at faithfully serving each other's needs in an understanding way, they may find the one with the initially higher desire is satisfied more easily than imagined. When a person feels like he is starving, all he can think about is when his next meal will come. When he knows that his next meal will be available when needed, he is able to think about other things. The person who has the lower sexual desire may find an increasing level of physical desire when other aspects – emotional and spiritual – of the marriage are improved. They also often find that romantic feelings follow romantic actions.

If a person's sexual appetite is outside these levels and is causing a problem in the marriage, Christian counseling/therapy is generally advised.

"For a while now, I haven't had much interest in sex. What are some of the factors that could be causing my low libido?"

Numerous factors can decrease a person's sex drive. Seek help if you may be impacted by any of the following and are unable to find freedom:

* Feeling hurt and angry toward your spouse
* Having an angry or controlling spouse
* Feeling incompetent as a person or a partner
* Fearing intimacy (childhood or past relationship experiences or feeling that intimacy reflects weakness)
* Negative body image
* Being a perfectionist and needing to be in control
* Being distracted or consumed by work or hobbies
* Depression, loss or grief that leaves you feeling numb
* Low testosterone (Both men and women have testosterone.)
* A husband's struggling to see his wife as a lover now that she is a mother to his children
* Sexual wounds from your past that have produced guilt and shame
* Use of pornography, compulsive masturbation and other distorted activities of sex addiction
* Side effects from medications such as antiandrogens, antiarrhythmics, anticancer agents, anticholinerics, antihistamines

(reduced vaginal lubrication), antihypertensives (erectile dysfunction or ED and libido), diuretics, hormones (e.g. corticosteroids, progestins), opiates, psychotropics (sedatives and stimulants can block dopamine receptors), antidepressants (reduced desire, ED and ejaculation difficulties), H_2 blockers (reduces testosterone metabolism), decongestants (ED), enlarged prostate medications (Proscar), contraceptives, etc. The possible impact of a drug depends on the individual involved, the drugs involved and the dosage. It can take up to six weeks for drug side effects to be revealed. (Be sure *not to* change medications without first talking to your health care provider.)

* Fatigue and stress
* Medical conditions (cardiovascular disease, hypertension, diabetes, anemia, MS, undetected thyroid disease and cancer)
* Peyronie's disease (a bowing of the penis that makes sex painful)
* Personality traits (worrier, anxious, ADD, OCD)
* Alcohol use by men (acts as a depressant and decreases arousal)[1]
* Hormonal changes due to obesity
* Fear of pregnancy
* Smoking, since nicotine decreases blood flow to key organs and reduces sperm quality.

If you suspect that one or more of the above-listed factors may be impacting your sex drive, visit your health care provider (physical and/or mental) to further explore causes and solutions.

"Is it ever okay to say 'No' to my spouse's request for sex?"

This question is best answered by thinking through motives and feelings. In marriage, both partners should be striving to find a middle ground where they can meet each other's physical needs and sexual desires. At times, saying "No" to a request for sex is fine and to be expected, because honestly, real life means there are times when someone is too tired, stressed or distracted. But saying "No" should be the rare exception rather than the rule.

In order to freely say "Yes" to sex, you also have to be able to freely say "No." But if you turn down a request for sex, be sure to state your reason why and offer an alternative time, preferably within the next day or so. Be careful not to shame your spouse or come across as rejecting him or her.

Also, if you do not have a reasonable reason for saying "No," yet you still really don't want to have sex, strive to have sex anyway. In other words, occasionally "take one for the team." You may be surprised at the positive results! It is not unusual for the person who initially wasn't interested to then discover the sex is quite enjoyable once things get going!

Don't resort to bartering ("I'll give you sex if you clean up the kitchen, stay with the kids while I go shopping, go to that work party with me, etc.") Also, don't use sex to manipulate your spouse. Sex is a God-ordained gift of connection for the two of you – not a tool of manipulation that you can wield on a whim to coerce your spouse into doing something or to cover up for ways you have been careless in other areas of the marriage.

"What are some ways that I can increase my desire for sex?"

In addition to dealing with relevant items listed above, consider trying the following:

1. Have sex every day for a few weeks, focusing primarily on the pleasure of the spouse who does not usually climax as easily. Give your emotions, body and hormones time to work together. The more your sexual response is stimulated, the better it works. Satisfying sex can serve as positive reinforcement for more bonding and intimacy.
2. Engage in extended foreplay, especially foreplay that is more playful in nature.
3. Look for additional ways to give and to receive physical affection while clothed.

"It's such a struggle for us to find the time and energy for love-making. Do you have any suggestions?"

Every healthy marriage includes healthy sexual intimacy. God designed us this way. Sex should be something that relaxes you, reduces stress and helps bring balance back into your life and marriage. It's not just a chore to be placed at the end for your "To- Do" list. If you're too busy for sex, you're too busy!

Based on 1 Corinthians 7:5, if you aren't having sex on a regular basis, something isn't right. Changes are needed. Sexual intercourse is a celebration of your marriage covenant that God instructs you to partake in regularly.

Cut some things out of your schedule, at least temporarily. Do that even if that involves your children's activities or church commitments. While it might not seem very romantic, scheduling sex, when necessary, on your calendar is wise. It's important – certainly as important as your son's basketball game or your neighborhood picnic, right? If you fail to take decisive action, your marriage will suffer, and you will eventually regret neglecting this vital part of your marriage.

"Ever since we had our first child, my interest in sex has all but disappeared. What's up with that?"

During pregnancy and the delivery of a child, your body went through dramatic changes physically and hormonally. You are adjusting to a lot, and much of it in those first months after delivery is beyond your control. Additionally, any remaining pregnancy weight can take its toll on you feeling sexy. That's normal.

Also, while breastfeeding your child is a great choice for your child's health and well-being, prolactin, the hormone that enables you to produce breast milk, temporarily reduces your sex drive. After weaning your baby and making time for some self-care and exercise, your libido should rebound.

Gently encourage your husband to be a part of your recovery too. If this is your first child, he probably doesn't realize the pre- and postpartum effects you have experienced. His not having been able to have sex with you, as you neared your due date and certainly for several weeks afterward, magnifies the differences in how you both are feeling. This is a critical time to work together as a team.

You don't need us to tell you that rearing a child takes a lot of time, attention and energy. It's draining to be on call 24/7/365. The time that you once enjoyed in abundance for each other now has to be carved out and scheduled in advance. Even a short weekend nap by yourself seems like a great treat.

While this is an especially challenging time for you both, this too shall pass. Keep your eye on your marriage though. Don't let the love that produced your baby be robbed by your baby. Taking the time to continue building your marriage is the best gift you can give your child. Be diligent to be affirming and affectionate toward one another throughout the day, and you likely will find it easier to sexually connect.

If you are feeling postpartum depression, see your doctor right away. Don't suffer through this alone. Help is available.

If as a husband you are having difficulty getting beyond the mental image of having seen your wife give birth, this is not uncommon. Many husbands admit that after having seen their baby born, they struggle with remembering their wife from a sexual perspective.

Resist the urge to shut down emotionally if you are having these struggles. Rather, remind yourself that your wife did not lose her sensuous nature because of childbirth. Recall with gladness the intensity and passion of your lovemaking. Continue to nurture all forms of intimacy with your wife, foster good communication and actively carve out time each day to be alone with her – even if it is some quiet time before you go to bed. As you both adjust to being parents, you also can simultaneously protect your intimate time together, including sex once she heals physically.

"Can I get pregnant while I am still nursing my baby?"

Yes, that is definitely possible. Even if you haven't started your menstrual period again, it is still possible to ovulate (release the egg from your ovary) and conceive. If you wish to lessen the risk of getting pregnant while nursing, use contraception.

"We are considering getting pregnant. How long can sperm remain viable after having sex?"

Sperm may live for up to three days. While you may not be ovulating at the time of intercourse, you may still become pregnant during the following 72 hours. Couples should keep this fact in mind if they are seeking, or wishing to avoid, pregnancy.

"Does the Bible prohibit intercourse during menstruation?"

In the Old Testament, ceremonial law prohibited intercourse during a woman's period. This law was given for both cleanliness and for spiritual purposes and was before the times of convenient bathing, showering and sanitary protection. In addition, the ceremonial law has been fulfilled by Christ per Hebrews 9 and 10; so today, if a couple wishes to engage sexually during the wife's period, they are free to do so.

You should be respectful, however, if either of you has reservations. Many wives have no interest in having sex while they are having their period, especially for the first few days when bleeding is heaviest. Also, some husbands would not find it appealing either. If one of you is not interested in making love at this time of the month, respond to such reservation with grace.

"Sexual intercourse has become painful for me. Should I be concerned?"

The World Health Organization reports that over 20 percent of women experience dyspareunia – painful intercourse – during some point in their lives. If this is a problem for you, try using a personal lubricant during sex and a vaginal moisturizer. Also try different positions to reduce pressure or irritation. If altering positions or limiting the intensity of thrusting doesn't solve the problem, there may be another cause, such as ovarian cysts, infections of the uterus or Fallopian tubes, scar tissue, endometriosis or fibroids that requires medical attention. There also are conditions known as vaginismus and vulvodynia.

Men also can experience pain during sex. Infections or other conditions in the penis, urethra, bladder, testicles or prostate can be the cause.

If you as a husband or wife are experience pain during sex, make a note as to when and where the pain occurs and discuss this with your doctor. Do not wait for conditions to "go away" on their own, particularly if the pain is present each time you have sex.

"Is it okay to fantasize about making love to someone other than my spouse? Will that make our love life more exciting?"

Some things can be exciting yet morally wrong at the same time. Fantasizing about someone other than your spouse is actually a form of lust that Jesus equated with adultery in Matthew 5:28. Bringing a third party into the most intimate part of your marriage, physically or virtually through our imagination or pornography, undermines true intimacy and involves just using your spouse's body with an ulterior motive.

You would be far better off fantasizing together about being in different settings you both find enjoyable and verbally sharing these fantasies with each other. That way, intimacy remains both exclusively pure and enjoyable.

Also, if you are going to fantasize about each other, make sure you are not unfairly imagining an "improved" version of your spouse. We don't nurture authentic sexual intimacy by closing our eyes and putting our spouse's face upon a body that doesn't look anything like his or hers.

"Does size matter?"

Due to social conditioning and a myth perpetuated by all those "male enhancement" Internet ads, some men are concerned about the size of their penis just as some women are concerned about the size of their breasts. Neither one needs to be concerned.

All that is needed for a husband to sexually satisfy his wife is about two to three inches of length. Most men will have an erection exceeding that, so there is no need for concern. God created the vagina to accommodate the typical six- to eight-inch erect penis. If excessive length is a problem, you can try alternate positions that reduce the depth of penetration.

Breast size is a matter of cultural conditioning and personal preference. Since all women's breasts contain about the same number of pleasure-creating nerve endings, the less-endowed woman will have a greater density of nerves and will typically be more easily stimulated by touch.

Wise couples will ignore cultural "standards of beauty" and enjoy their spouse, just the way God created him or her. Ultimately, it's not the size that matters. It's learning what to do with it to build awesome sexual connection.

"Where can a Christian go to get help with a sexual problem?"

First, a word of advice regarding counseling that especially applies to sexual issues. While most competent counselors can provide some helpful advice, a non-Christian counselor doesn't have knowledge of the revealed Word of God and could recommend a course of treatment that is contrary to Scripture. This is something you should be aware of and avoid if possible.

> *"Blessed is the man who walks not in*
> *the counsel of the wicked."*

(Psalm 1:1, ESV)

In addition to the spiritual views of the counselor, be sure to check the counselor's training, professional qualifications and certifications, and that the person's advice isn't in conflict with Scripture. With regard to sexual issues, there are therapists who may even recommend the use of pornography to "spice things up." That's just bad advice on so many levels. See Chapter 14 for additional resources.

"What advice do you have regarding how to discuss sexual issues with my spouse? I'm afraid I might offend them and make matters worse."

Talking about sexual issues can be a sensitive topic for couples because sex is so intertwined with how a couple views themselves and their relationship. Handled well, talking about sex can open up exciting new avenues of understanding and marital intimacy. If handled poorly, lasting pain and frustration can result. Clearly, this is an area needing direction from the Holy Spirit.

In addition to suggestions we made in Chapter 7, following are additional suggestions:

Begin with prayer and self-examination. Are your motives pure and unselfish? Are you driven by a desire to serve your spouse and strengthen your marriage? Have you been working on the other areas of your marriage, such as love and respect?

Express your appreciation for your spouse's love and state your desire to work together on building your marriage. Ask your spouse if this is a good time to discuss your matter of concern.

Discuss one topic at a time and clearly state what you would like to see done differently in your sexual relationship. Also share how you personally may have contributed directly (by your actions or words) or indirectly (by your attitude or avoidance). Express what you are willing to do differently. Be extra careful not to come across as condescending or feeling superior.

Brainstorm ways that you could both contribute to improving your relationship. Pick one of the ways to which you are both open and try it out for a while.

Pray. Prayerfully commit to continuing to discuss your sexual relationship in a loving manner.

"Is oral sex okay for a married or unmarried Christian couple?"

The Bible does not explicitly address this subject, so a married Christian couple should apply the four biblical principles regarding sex to this question.

Some conservative Christians consider oral sex to be sodomy, even though the word *sodomy* doesn't appear in the Bible and wasn't coined until nearly 400 A.D. Even then, the word *sodomy* was defined only as anal sex between two men, consistent with the teaching of the Apostle Paul in Romans 1:21-32. Several centuries later, a church leader by the name of Benedict Levita, broadened the definition of the word *sodomy* to include *"any* sexual act unrelated to procreation," in keeping with the thinking of the Middle Ages.

Other Christian teachers believe that Bible verses such as Song of Songs 2:3, 4:16 and 7:2, 8, 9 indicate that Solomon and his wife engaged in oral sex with the blessing of God since this book is part of Scripture. Passages that seem to indicate this practice are those that describe the wife's body parts in a progression leading from her face to her genitals and then describing their desire as being like eating fruits and drinking wine. The implication of oral sex in such a discreet manner would seem consistent with the sensitivities of the day and also prevent such an intimate exchange between this newlywed couple from voyeuristic, public consumption.

Another argument that speaks to the acceptability of oral sex is more of a logical nature. For example, if we can reasonably argue it is not wrong for a husband to kiss his wife's breasts or for a wife to kiss her husband's neck, then it's reasonable that the genitals also are not off limits. In other words, there is no literal or arbitrary line on the body that would tell us we can rightfully be on one side of it but not on the other.

If both of you feel comfortable with oral sex without being pressured to do so, we do not see anything biblically that would prohibit this as a part of your foreplay and lovemaking repertoire.

That said, some health considerations would make oral sex ill-advised for anyone who has or may have been infected from previous sexual relations with HPV or another STD/STI. In recent years, there has been an alarming increase in cancer of the mouth, neck and head, due to exposure to certain strains of HPV. If either of you had sexual relations outside of your marriage, be sure to discuss getting tested first with your doctors. You owe it to each other to do so.

As an added precaution, avoid oral sex when you have cuts or sores on your mouth or genitals. Avoid flossing or brushing your teeth directly prior to or after oral sex since bleeding gums can increase your risk of infection.

Unmarried couples should realize that oral sex *is* sex, and doing so outside of marriage is fornication. As I have already mentioned, I (Julie) occasionally speak on abstinence to middle school and high school students. Many teenagers try to argue that they can participate in oral sex while still "technically" remaining pure. I always tell them that is shaky reasoning, considering that one half of the phrase "oral sex" is the word "sex." I also ask the young people, "When you are married, will you be fine with your spouse giving oral sex to or receiving oral sex from someone else?" Obviously, they then begin to see that "oral sex" is indeed "sex."

Suffice it to say, many married couples find that oral sex adds variety and additional pleasure to their lovemaking. If you are concerned about cleanliness or odors, simply take the time to shower or wash your genital area before being intimate. You may also want to use a flavored lubricant or edible powder for variety. Following these guidelines will lessen your concerns and allow you to focus more on the pleasure of giving and receiving oral sex.

If you decide oral sex has a place in your sexual intimacy, we encourage you to take a reciprocal approach, meaning you both get to give and receive. If it becomes a situation where one person always wants to receive but is unwilling to give – or one person is willing to give but never wants to receive – we doubt it will be as bonding of an experience as it could be if it was more mutual.

"What about anal intercourse?"

While the Bible doesn't directly address this topic for married heterosexual couples, it is a sex act that carries with it its own unique risks. A couple would definitely need to hold it up to the four scriptural principles outlined earlier in this chapter before determining if it has a place in their lovemaking. Additionally, couples should be aware of significant health risks and practical considerations with regard to anal intercourse.

The anus and immediate surrounding areas often carry dangerous bacteria, viruses such as HPV and intestinal parasites. Anal intercourse followed by vaginal intercourse is dangerous due to bacterial and viral contamination and obviously should be avoided. The World Health Organization refers to anal intercourse as *"a high risk human sexual activity."*

While some may argue that the Bible doesn't explicitly disallow anal intercourse for married heterosexual couples, the inspired words of the Apostle Paul would certainly apply for the health risks alone.

> *"I have the right to do anything," you say--but not everything is beneficial. "I have the right to do anything"--but not everything is constructive."*

> (1 CORINTHIANS 10:23)

The anus does not provide any lubrication when stimulated. Without proper lubrication, there is a heightened risk of skin abrasion and infection, including STDs. Even condoms can be more susceptible to leakage, breakage, and slippage during anal intercourse than with vaginal intercourse, adding to the health risks. Could it be that the lack of lubrication is an indication that God didn't intend for people to engage sexually in this manner?

Rectal tissues are fragile, and unlike the vagina, they aren't very elastic. As a result, the wife is more susceptible to tearing, producing abscesses and rupturing hemorrhoids. These raise the risk of infection and other medical problems, such as weakening the sphincter muscle (making it harder to hold feces) even further.

For health, religious and cultural reasons, anal intercourse is considered taboo or unnatural in many parts of the world, and the practice is illegal in some countries.

Granted, the tightness of the anus around a penis would be greater than what vaginal intercourse provides, but getting used to that degree of tightness can reduce a husband's interest and pleasure from the sensations of vaginal sex, and that result would be tragic. Research has shown that most women who have been put in this undesirable and potentially unhealthy position didn't find anal intercourse to be enjoyable.

Nearly every husband who requests anal sex will receive a "No" from his wife. We believe she would be justified in her reservation, concern and denial. Love needs to be at the foundation of every marriage, and it's obviously not loving to pressure your wife on this issue of anal sex when she says, "No."

If your husband is requesting anal sex, it could be that he occasionally desires more intense sensations that come with firmer pressure on the head of his penis. As a couple, explore other ways to satisfy this need through the use of your hands or oral sex. You as a wife can also tighten your PC muscles during intercourse, which can create a pleasurable sensation for both of you.

For most couples, anal sex misses the primary purpose of the mutual celebration of oneness in their marriage. Having your wife lovingly embrace your penis with her vagina is a profound reminder and celebration of God's bringing you together to both enjoy one another. Therefore, we would strongly caution couples against engaging in anal intercourse.

"We're getting older. When should we stop having sex?"

Stop? Why? Intercourse can and should continue as long as you are both healthy enough for sex. While some couples may need to make adjustments due to health issues including lack of natural lubrication or painful intercourse, you are never too old to feel physical pleasure. Speak to your doctor if sex becomes physically painful, causes bleeding or if erectile dysfunction becomes problematic.

Contrary to the assumption that sex just fades away as a couple ages, some married couples report that the sex actually gets better in their later years. This could be because they are beyond the stress of raising a family and struggling financially and now have more time to spend with each other. Or possibly they finally shed the inhibitions or skewed theology that plagued their sexual intimacy earlier in their marriage.

If intercourse becomes impossible, look for other ways to nurture physical intimacy in your marriage. Redeveloping your sexual style as a couple may include focusing more on other forms of touch (holding hands, hugging, kissing, backrubs or whole body massage), showering or bathing together or using manual, oral or vibrator stimulation to arousal or orgasm for either or both of you.

Be wise. Having a "100-percent-of-the-time" intercourse performance standard will eventually lead to the avoidance of sex. Believing that it's "intercourse or nothing" likely will result in "nothing." Continue working on your overall marriage. Healthy, creative spouses who connect deeply are more likely to enjoy satisfying sexual pleasure well into their 80s through playful intimacy.

GOING DEEPER TOGETHER

1. Discuss any new insights from this chapter that might be beneficial in your marriage. What changes would you like to make, if any?
2. Discuss Initiating and Responding to Sexual Intimacy
   a. Identify two ways you like to initiate sexual connection.
   b. What are your two favorite ways that your spouse can invite you to connect sexually with him or her? What facilitates anticipation and desire for you?
   c. Share openly with each other and seek to reach agreement on the initiating and receiving parts of your couple sexual style.
3. Schedule some time for extended lovemaking. Be sure that you are both rested, relaxed and have eliminated interruptions. Do this on a regular basis so that sex isn't always at the

end of your "To-Do" list. Scheduling time may not sound "romantic," but scheduling sex is a necessity for about 80 percent of couples.

4. Read a good Christian book on sex together. Alternate reading a few pages out loud. Some recommended books can be found on our website, http://pursuitofpassionbook.com.

CHAPTER 9

Protecting Intimacy in Your Marriage

§

WHETHER YOU ARE ENGAGED OR newly married, it may be hard for you to fathom that there will ever be a time when something could come between the two of you and cause pain and resentment.

All married couples, though, at some point realize that *falling* in love is not the same as *staying* in love. More importantly, they realize that building a healthy and strong marriage is as much about daily choices and commitment as it is about love.

Our hope is that you don't want just an "okay" marriage, but that you genuinely want a great marriage. As much as we would like to say those feelings of love are enough to get you there, they aren't.

What we will tell you enthusiastically, though, is that if you both commit to consistently protecting your intimacy (sexual, emotional and spiritual), you will together build something incredibly enriching.

Much in our society rails against boundaries that will protect your intimacy. Nowhere is this more evident than in the realm of sex. You wouldn't have to look hard to find messages that sexual promiscuity even among married people is "normal" or "acceptable." Sexual activity that once was considered "fringe" behavior, such as swinging (couples swapping partners) and group sex, has become more mainstream than many people realize.

As a woman who blogs about sex, I (Julie) have had several discussions with other women about sexual intimacy. It is not unusual for me to occasionally hear about suburban neighborhoods where spouse swapping is increasingly common. I have also listened to women who wonder if they should submit to their husband's desire to invite another woman or man into their marriage bed with them.

You may assume such conversations are happening with non-believers who do not have a biblical gauge that promotes the exclusivity of the husband and wife bond. Sadly, some of these conversations have been with Christian wives – women who from all imaginable standpoints are not much different than you and me as wives.

As if this increasingly weakened footing isn't bad enough, we must also consider the impact of the onslaught of pornography. Explicit and unrealistic pictures and videos of sex and particularly of women have become increasingly easy to access. It is no wonder our society has lost its moral compass that would readily keep us on a path of sexual integrity. Pornography can range from what some people would describe as mild depictions of people having illicit sex to brutal portrayals of sexual violence. Pornography can show up digitally (such as in pictures or videos on computers, tablets and phones), as well as in print form in magazines or pamphlets.

Adult entertainment venues, where customers pay to view other people nude or in sexually charged positions, are a thriving business in many cities and even small towns.

Within the United States and globally, the sex trade – where young girls in particular are sold as a commodity for sex – is a horrendous crisis that contributes to the skewed view of sex.

Of course, everyday advertising is one of the most common exposures we have to sexual suggestion. Traipse through your local shopping mall, and you will see many storefronts showing lingerie or revealing clothing, usually with a heightened emphasis on a woman's breasts, legs and body curves. Open a magazine and glossy inserts with sensuous-looking models advertising perfume may scatter across your floor.

Even nighttime comedies that air in what were once deemed family-friendly timeslots are laden with blatant and subtle sexual scenes and innuendoes. Ours has become a society defined in part by casual sex to the point that it is almost impossible to discern healthy sexual intimacy. It's not just that the lines are blurry. In many cases, there are no lines.

The sheer amount of tainted messages we receive about sex should alert us to the need to protect and honor intimacy within our marriages. In fact, the degree to which we see sex and sexuality misused on a grand societal scale should be a vibrant reminder of the other extreme – that sex is sacred and worthy of protection in its right and holy context of marriage.

Make no mistake; it will be increasingly difficult for you to set boundaries that protect your sexual intimacy if you don't set such boundaries intentionally and regularly.

Sounds daunting, doesn't it? To a degree, it is. *But* the good news is that if you do set some boundaries, you will be well on your way to that strong and healthy marriage we mentioned earlier in this chapter.

How to Protect Intimacy in Your Marriage

1. Have sex often and learn how to enjoy it.
This point may seem like an obvious one to bring up, but if the two of you have sex often and you both enjoy it, then sex will become vitally woven into the fabric of your marriage. You will be less likely to entertain thoughts or actions that will diminish or destroy your relationship.

Diligently watch for those experiences of married life that can take a toll on your sexual time together. The demands of parenting, work, extended family obligations, ministry and maintaining a home can leave a couple wondering if they will ever get alone time with each other.

> *"The average married couple spends just four minutes a day alone together."*
>
> ~ Sari Harrar & Rita DeMaria, Ph.D.,
> authors of *The 7 Stages of Marriage*

The truth is that you won't get that time – unless you make it a priority. What it means in a practical sense is that you may have to say "No, not at this time," more often to volunteer opportunities at your kids' school or at church. You may have to occasionally push the unfolded laundry off the bed so that you can make love. You may have to raise your tolerance for a home that is more cluttered than you would prefer.

At the end of the day, though, you have to ask yourself what is best for your marriage – having a house that looks like the inside spread of a *Good Housekeeping* magazine or feeling truly connected to the person you married?

Consistent and enjoyable sex may not get you "Volunteer of the Year" awards in the community or church, but it will get you connection with your spouse. And ultimately, that's better for you, your spouse, your kids, your community and your church.

2. BE HONEST AND TRANSPARENT ABOUT YOUR NEEDS.
Possibly nothing does more to kill intimacy than to assume our spouse knows what we need – or to assume we know what they need.

Your marriage should be the safest place for you to express your needs (sexual and otherwise). Sadly, some married couples have not made their marriage a safe haven. Instead of two people who have the assurance to come transparently to each other, we find two people who have individually isolated themselves emotionally. The stresses of life tend to fuel this isolation, as each person goes to his or her separate corner to simply toughen up and "get through" the day (or week or month or year!)

Mark our words on this one – individually isolating when life gets chaotic and stressful will become your unhealthy norm if you don't intentionally build healthier patterns.

I (Julie) remember a date night with Randall where we had the opportunity to talk about what stress was doing to our marriage. I remember clearly saying to him, "I need the hard things of life to drive us together, not drive us apart."

I wish I could say that all it took was that one conversation to cement in place a deep tendency to be transparent with each other. Nope. Those healthy patterns began to take hold only after multiple times of being vulnerable with each other about what we each specifically needed. Taking those intentional steps has paid off. Though we still can slip into a mode of isolation, we are now more likely to be open about what we each need.

By "needs," we're talking about anything from the practical aspects of life ("I need more help with the laundry.") to the more intricate aspects of your relationship ("I need some alone time with you," or "I need to make love to you."). Will you each always be able to meet the other's needs? No. However, if you each bend your heart toward sacrificial and abundant love, you will find that more often than not, you will have a growing desire to meet each other's needs. Train your heart in that direction, and that goal will become the tendency of your heart.

When two people get married, a prime reason is because they have found someone with whom they want to journey through life together. What good is journeying together if you're really doing it apart? See the irony?

Do you want great sex in your marriage? Get good at being transparent about expressing what you need, and be slow in becoming defensive or indifferent when your spouse expresses what he or she needs.

3. BE YOUR SPOUSE'S FRIEND.

This suggestion seems like just a redundant repeat of the previous point, right? Well, it does actually build on the second point but is still worthy of its own attention.

Sometimes, people will ask us what leads to a strong healthy marriage. You may think that because this book is about sex, we will automatically answer, "Sex!"

Obviously, we think sex is vital to a healthy marriage, but another ingredient that is more foundational is friendship. (And friendship actually makes the sex better too, so it's a win-win all the way around!)

Unfortunately, some husbands and wives have little friendship with each other, yet they seem to have ample friendships with other people.

Have you ever noticed how some women treat their female friends better than they treat their own husbands? They speak more respectively to them, laugh more with them, and listen more attentively when something is troubling them. Have you ever noticed how some men treat their guy buddies better than they treat their wives? They joke around with them more, go out of their way to help them more, show them respect, and are always looking for opportunities to do things with them.

We are not saying that a couple shouldn't have friends outside their marriage. What we are saying is that you should be best friends with each other within your marriage.

Protect your intimacy by intentionally nurturing your friendship with each other and enjoying each other's company, insight and conversation.

4. AT LEAST SOME OF THE TIME, ALLOW YOUR SPOUSE TO SEE YOU NAKED AND MAKE LOVE WITH THE LIGHTS ON.
Have you ever felt self-conscious about your body? If so, you are not alone. It is not unusual for women to struggle with body image, especially as the effects of childbearing and aging naturally impact outward appearance. Men also can struggle with their physical appearance. To fully enjoy your sexual relationship, you will need to develop a positive appreciation of your body and your spouse's body as well.

When it comes to sex, some people just refuse to allow their spouse to see their naked body. If you want to protect and strengthen your intimacy, though, we encourage you to resist the urge to hide your body from your spouse. Become more comfortable being naked with each other and actually seeing each other's bodies.

The reason so many people struggle with body image is because they compare their bodies with those of people in the modeling and entertainment industries. News flash, right?! Not exactly. Even though we know that what we see on the screen or in print has been professionally created and/or digitally manipulated, we still can easily struggle with the comparisons.

We wish we could tell you that the media and Hollywood will at some point start presenting more realistic representations of appearance. That would be nice, but it's not likely.

A better approach for your marriage is to stop waiting for society to change and instead embrace a healthy attitude about your body and your spouse's body. Work on those areas you can change and learn to accept those things that you can't change. In other words, make peace with your body.

We know that most Christian women particularly strive to be modest. Modesty has its place, but that place is primarily when being around other people. Too much modesty in your private moments with your spouse, however, can be detrimental to your marriage.

In the privacy of your relationship and certainly within the exclusivity of your lovemaking, appreciate and affirm each other's body. Occasionally, make love with some light in the room, whether it is the soft light of a candle or a nightstand lamp. If you have a light in your closet, consider turning it on and opening the closet door slightly so light streams into the room. And certainly don't rule out sex during the day, when natural sunlight can illuminate the room.

Allow your spouse to undress you and take the initiative to undress him or her. Undressing each other can be a sensuous aspect of foreplay.

Seeing each other's bodies will not only help you associate sexual arousal with your spouse, it also will reinforce the power of visual stimulation. Research shows that men are incredibly visual and that husbands desire to see their wife's body. Sadly, too many wives rob their husbands of this experience, insisting instead to make love "with the lights out and the covers pulled up." Don't be that kind of wife! Be a wife who encourages her husband to visually partake of her body.

If you are a wife who struggles with seeing your husband's naked body, consider this: when you enjoy and appreciate your husband's naked body, there is less of a tendency to see sex as dirty or wrong. In the right context of marital sexual intimacy, we can appreciate that our bodies in their entirety are good, beautiful and holy.

5. BLOCK ACCESS TO PORNOGRAPHY OR OTHER INTERACTIONS THAT COULD COMPROMISE INTIMACY IN YOUR MARRIAGE.

Do you know that some people inadvertently expose themselves to porn by typing in something rather innocent on a Google search that just happens to have a "key word" that is associated with sex?

Of course, some people intentionally go online looking for pornography.

Either way pornography enters your life can have a damaging and/or destructive effect on your intimacy.

One way to limit the influx of sexually explicit material into your home and heart is to stop it from reaching the screen of your computer, phone or tablet. Available filtering software programs will do exactly that. See Chapter 14 for some suggestions.

If you find yourself struggling with wanting to look at pornography or even if you accidentally stumble across pornographic material, tell your spouse. The obvious reason for honesty in this matter is because you want accountability between each other, and you want to get in the healthy habit of being quick to shed light on issues that could potentially do serious damage to your relationship if left unchecked.

A less obvious reason is that spiritually, Satan is always looking to exploit cracks in the foundation of your marriage. The enemy hates marriage because God designed it. Satan's go-to method is always division (which we can readily see in not only how he goes after marriages, but also family relationships, work relationships, friendships and so forth).

Satan works in the dark, and by that we mean that he thrives on our human nature to hide or keep secret anything that could be perceived as a moral failing. Some of you may be thinking, "But what about the people appearing in pornographic material? They seem to be open about it."

To this question we would say that many people in the pornography industry are open about it only with other people in the industry, so there is no sense of a moral failing. If you ask many of those same people if they are equally open about their profession with their parents, grandparents and childhood friends, most of them would deny such openness.

Satan works in the dark world of secrecy, lies and cover-ups.

God works in the light. The more you shed light into temptations and behaviors that are destructive to your marriage, the less power you give to Satan – and the more power you give to God to heal and protect those areas.

GOING DEEPER TOGETHER

1. Of the five suggested ways to protect intimacy in your marriage, which one is the most challenging for you to apply? Discuss ways in which you can help each other strengthen your defense in that area.
2. Schedule a weekly time for intentionally investing in your marriage by communicating, developing your friendship and discussing your needs.

CHAPTER 10

Maintaining Intimacy as New Parents

MAINTAINING INTIMACY AND PASSION IN a marriage after the arrival of a child takes your concentrated effort, time and energy. Having a child – especially the first one – will dramatically change the atmosphere in your home, so you will both need to be intentional in order to succeed in the intimacy department.

Common challenges you will face as new parents include decreased energy, a busy and less predictable schedule, split emotional connections and eventually, reduced privacy. As a new mom, you also will probably have to deal with reduced sexual desire due to your hormonal changes, nursing and negative feelings about your body image.

As *Parents* magazine described it,

"Making the leap from coupledom to baby-makes-three is exciting, exhilarating, and wonderful. It's also exhausting, exasperating, and worrisome – a combination that can be toxic to the romantic relationship that made you parents in the first place."[1]

It's important to remember that your marriage needs to last far longer than the time you are rearing children, so be careful not to neglect your marriage relationship. Ultimately, the best gift you can give to your child is a mom and a dad with a strong marriage.

MAKE NECESSARY ADJUSTMENTS

Plan on making some adjustments to your schedule and in the expectations you have for your marriage, at least for the first year or two. While about 80 percent of couples report being *less* satisfied with their marriage after their baby is born, you can redevelop marital satisfaction through careful planning and honest communication.

FOR NEW PARENTS

Enlist the help of a family member; trade babysitting with another couple or get someone you trust from your church to enable you to get some time away as a couple. Spend some overnights away before the child is likely to experience separation anxiety (8 to 12 months of age).[2]

Keep dating each other but when you go out, restrain yourself from talking about your child. Save those discussions for times when you together are at home. Set aside time in your schedule to engage in some fun activities that you both enjoyed before the baby arrived. Try to be creative, flexible and realistic.

Be extra cautious about how you handle conflict in front of your child, even when he is an infant. Children can sense when their surroundings are filled with tension, even at a very young age.

Schedule time for sex. We know, it doesn't sound romantic, but making time is vital to the health of your marriage and will help keep your marriage strong. As soon as possible, keep your bedroom baby-free (at least at bedtime). You need to preserve some space that is exclusively yours for love and romance.

Be prepared for a second child too. Having a second child is likely to be just as big an adjustment as having the first one!

FOR FATHERS

One of the most important things you as a father can do for your children is to faithfully love your wife. Avoid having a "pity party" if you have to be a bit more patient regarding the frequency of sex. This too shall pass – especially if you and your wife keep the lines of communication open and nurture intimacy. Also, be on guard against the temptation to use pornography. Satan loves to attack dads, especially during this time.

Help your wife fight the urge to "do it all." Learn all that you can about caring for your child. Look for ways to sacrificially help lighten your wife's load around the house and provide some alone time for her. Doing what is referred to as "choreplay" will go a long way in helping you and your wife get back to the sex life you desire, once she and her doctor give the okay.

Look for ways to rekindle the romance in your marriage once things begin to settle down, and your wife is ready for it. Make all of the arrangements for your dates, even if it is after you discuss date options together. Consider buying your wife something special to wear on your date, if you know her style preferences, size, etc. With patience and understanding, romance can return to your marriage.

Encourage your wife and reassure her that she is a capable and competent mother. Since she is likely to have fewer adult interactions for a while, spend time engaging in adult conversation more than usual. Help her to stay connected to what is happening outside your home. Your wife needs adult conversation and engagement that might otherwise be in short supply.

Having a child highlights our tendency toward selfishness. It also provides many opportunities to "die to yourself" and serve the needs of your family. As a man of honor, let go of some of your personal goals in order to be there for your wife and child.

> *"Husbands, love your wives, just as Christ loved*
> *the church and gave himself up for her...."*

(EPHESIANS 5:25)

FOR MOTHERS
If you ask your husband for help, unless there is a direct threat do life or limb, give him the freedom to do things his way. If you are unwilling to do that, then be fair and keep the chore for yourself. This is a time to refocus on respecting your husband. He wants to help you, so be extra careful not to criticize his efforts. His approach might not be as well-informed as yours might be, but your child will probably survive, and your marriage will be better off if you're gentle in correcting him.

Express your appreciation for his working to provide for your family. Both of your lives are now filled with more responsibility, and he will be encouraged to hear your words of affirmation, especially when he is facing stress at work.

While you have been focused on your child, his needs for sex have probably been on hold. He is likely to greatly appreciate it if you initiate non-vaginal sex with him at this time and reassure him that you still desire him sexually. Once you have your doctor's approval, reintegrate sexual intercourse into your lovemaking.

If your church has a new moms' group, get involved in it. Look for a mom with more experience than you have as a mother, and ask her to be a mentor for you.

Whether you are a stay-at-home mother or one who also works outside of the home, the reality is that when a child arrives, our expectations have to shift with regard to what realistically can get done. If you become consumed with having a perfectly kept house, a rigorous schedule and a pace that you kept before you had your baby, you will likely find yourself frustrated and disappointed.

Read Proverbs 31. Some readers have mistakenly thought that the woman in this passage was a "superwoman" and did all of the tasks listed by herself and all at the same time. The reality is, this account looks back over the course of her entire adult life. The secret of her success was that she prioritized and managed her responsibilities and her interests differently, during the various stages of her life. She also married a "Proverbs 31 man" who had confidence in her (vs. 11), encouraged her (vs. 28) and built a strong marriage with her (vs. 12).

The best thing you can do for your child is to provide him a stable home with a mom and dad who love each other. When you see the value in this priority, you will likely loosen your grip on building the "perfect" life.

Your child needs to see that "dad" and "mom" are first and foremost "husband" and "wife." Continue to show your husband affection – even an occasional passionate kiss or playful sensuous touch – in front of your children. Don't let sexual intimacy drift out of your relationship; rather, nurture it with intention and a heartfelt desire to honor God and your husband.

"Having a child intensifies everything in a relationship. With the arrival of a first child, everything good in a marriage gets better, everything bad gets worse. A couple that has good intimacy will find a lot more to share, more experiences to get excited about together. A couple that has a lot of distance will find that a child becomes a wedge." [3]

~ JERROLD L. SHAPIRO, PhD, PSYCHOLOGIST

GOING DEEPER TOGETHER

1. Identify three fun activities you both enjoy doing that don't cost any (or much) money. Schedule them for days during the coming month and mark them on your calendar.
2. Discuss how having a baby changed your responsibilities at home. What specific outside responsibilities or activities will need to be suspended or eliminated?

3. What are each of your three greatest needs right now? Discuss how you can address those with each other. Then repeat this exercise at least annually.

CHAPTER 11

Limiting the Possibility of an Affair

§

EVERY CHRISTIAN'S MARRIAGE IS INTENDED to be a visible representation of Christ's love for His Church (Ephesians 5:32). While God
designed marriage to be that way, couples can easily get off track if
they let down their guard.

We wish we could tell you that you can "affair proof" your marriage. A marriage, however, is made up of two individuals, and each
has the free will to make healthy or unhealthy choices that impact
the other person.

There are examples of spouses who did everything right "by the
book" – meaning they obeyed God's commands with regard to marriage, were available emotionally and sexually to their spouse, and
were faithful – yet their spouse still committed adultery. These situations grieve our hearts.

Even though we don't like the words "affair proof," we do believe
ardently that active steps can be taken to greatly limit the possibility
of an emotional or sexual affair. Nurturing sex in your marriage is
definitely part of that course of action. After all, one of the reasons
God purposely tells married couples to have sex often is to guard
against temptation (1 Corinthians 7:5).

Here are some ways to protect your marriage from adultery:

Recognize the Threat

Never assume that infidelity couldn't happen to you. People who naively disregard the risk are less likely to recognize the need to build and maintain protective measures in the marriage and with others.

> *"Be alert and of sober mind. Your enemy the devil prowls around like a roaring lion looking for someone to devour."*
>
> (1 Peter 5:8)

This isn't about being paranoid or not trusting your spouse. Rather, it's about having a discerning heart that is well-tuned to recognize strengths and weaknesses in your bond.

Take Action

Your best defense against an affair is a strong offense. Your marriage is sacred in God's eyes (and we hope in yours as well). It's worthy of your heart and devotion – not just in your words at the altar, but in your daily choices that build and enrich the relationship. Intentionally nurture your marriage on a regular basis – spiritually, emotionally, relationally and physically.

In my years as a speaker and writer, one common thread I (Julie) have seen is that unhealthy patterns in a marriage are usually unintentional, while healthy patterns are intentional. In other words, as a marriage is beginning, no one thinks or says, *"Someday I'm just going to take my spouse for granted and not put much effort into our relationship."*

Yet that's exactly where a couple drifts if they do not actively pursue a strong relationship.

If you and your spouse intentionally build those healthy patterns in big ways and small ways, your marriage likely will be characterized by trust, faithfulness and enjoyment of each other's company.

While we do not know exactly what will work for your marriage, we are confident some of the following ideas will help you build that strong offense against an affair:

SPIRITUALLY

1. Make your marriage your top priority after God – ahead of your job, children, parents, ministry and hobbies.
2. Pray together and ask God if there is anything in your life that needs attention or change.
3. Keep your relationship with the Lord current. A hardened heart spiritually leads to a vulnerable heart emotionally and once you begin down that road, it gets more difficult to turn back.
4. If possible, occasionally serve in a ministry together too.

EMOTIONALLY AND RELATIONALLY

1. In 1 Corinthians 7, we are told that *"If you marry, you will have many trials."* Plan on it happening to you! While each marriage is unique, it's also true that every marriage faces many of the same issues. After all, you are two sinners trying to figure out how to do life together, and that's not always easy.

Learn how to communicate and resolve conflict well. People with healthy marriages have mastered these skills. Forgive quickly and keep short accounts with each other (Ephesians 4:26).

2. Build accountability relationships with godly, mature same-gender friends and mentors in your life. Invite them to ask you tough questions about your integrity, character and commitments. We can't emphasize this enough that if you each have mature believers with whom you can be real on a regular basis, you will be less likely to venture down a path that will compromise your marriage. Men need male accountability partners, and women need female accountability partners.

3. Learn to recognize when temptation is approaching and develop the habit of disciplining your eyes, your mind and your heart. These are the three walls of protection that God has given us. Use them!

4. Watch any use of alcohol – especially among a mixed group of friends. Alcohol can cloud your judgment.

5. Be careful about the television programs and movies that you watch. Regularly watching lax moral attitudes and behaviors will numb your conscience and convictions.

6. Be aware of the threat that social media can be. If you don't have a shared account with your spouse, be sure that your own profile clearly indicates that you are married. Give each other all passwords and login information and complete access to your email and social accounts at any time without prior notification.

7. Do not use email, texting or social media to share that you are having marital problems. Instead, if you need to talk to someone, limit your conversations to private verbal

interactions with your accountability partners – the two or three safe friends who will offer insights and guidance that reflect God's Word and attitude about marriage.

8. Don't share any personal or private information that should be kept exclusively for your spouse. Never privately communicate with former love interests.

9. Maintain a work-family balance that you and your spouse can agree with, and spend meaningful time with your mate on a regular basis. Don't let an overloaded schedule rob you of quality *and* quantity time together, so you can build your marriage (Ephesians 4:3).

10. Maintain your friendship as a couple. Schedule time for activities that you each enjoy. Balance both "we" time and "me" time.

11. Annually attend a marriage seminar, join a marriage class at church and/or get a Christian marriage book and read it aloud to each other.

12. Keep your relationship growing and interesting. Go away for an overnight without the kids – or send the kids on one of their own with trusted relatives or family friends. Do something you both enjoyed when you were dating.

13. Speak up! If a friendship that your spouse has with someone else leaves you feeling uncomfortable, say so. Don't be enslaved by jealousy or fear, but do trust your intuition.

14. Learn how to grant and receive forgiveness. Every couple will need to do this often (Ephesians 4:32).

15. Cherish her; admire him. Love and respect are more than a feeling. They are an act of the will. Both love and respect should be given unconditionally. God's Word never attaches conditions on either one.

16. Burned out? Feelings often follow actions. Begin acting in loving, respectful ways toward each other, and the feelings will return.

17. Get help early. Marital problems rarely get better on their own with time. A skilled mentor or a Christian counselor can help you build a great marriage, and that's the best protection from an affair!

PHYSICALLY

1. Be physically affectionate with each other, regardless of whether you are in your home, public or social gatherings. Obviously, if you are around other people, your affection need not to be overtly sexual (although shared secret meanings between the two of you of what certain touches really mean can be fun!)

   Every couple has different feelings about "public display of affection" (PDA), but in general if you can build into your relationship a healthy amount of hand holding, hugging and appropriate touching, the better. Teach each other what you like. Don't assume. I (Julie) would remind Randall early in our marriage how much I like it when he puts his hand on my back or holds my hand when we are in public. He on his own wouldn't have known this had I not intentionally pointed it out. Now he is more conscientious of how much I like PDA!

2. Watch what you wear in public so as to draw attention to your face. Not surprisingly, wives need to be more aware of this than men because women's clothing is often designed to draw attention to her breasts and legs. We're not saying you can't dress fashionably or femininely. You can be stylish

without being seductive. There's a difference, and you serve your marriage well when you embrace that difference (1 Corinthians 6:18-20).

3. Have sex often and enjoy it. God designed sex to be a celebration of your oneness and marriage covenant. Learn how to please each other sexually. Learn how to embrace all the positive effects of sex. Then practice regularly (1 Corinthians 7:3-5).

Know the Warning Signs That Could Make an Affair More Likely

- Growing cold or apathetic – spiritually, emotionally, relationally or physically – with your spouse or your roles in life
- Looking forward to seeing or sharing your heart with anyone of the opposite sex (Flee from emotional adultery.)
- Daydreaming or dwelling on thoughts about someone of the opposite gender
- Not being the kind of person YOU would want to be married to
- Failing to resolve conflicts leading to bitterness and apathy
- Having conversations with others that involve issues you should be discussing only with your spouse (Relying too heavily on the advice of others, especially when such advice impacts your marriage and seems to purposely exclude the insights or opinions of your spouse.)
- Focusing more time and energy on your children than on your marriage (The best gift you can give your children is to build your marriage. This will be most difficult to comprehend when they are young and require a tremendous amount of your time and energy. Begin, though, when they are babies

to show them and yourselves that your strong marriage is vitally important to the stability of the family.)

* Working long hours so you don't have to spend as much time at home
* Doubting what God has already said in His Word regarding your marriage covenant
* Being especially careful when you are *"BLASTed"* (Bored, Lonely, Angry, Stressed or Tired).

GOING DEEPER TOGETHER

1. Work together on developing a set of boundaries for protecting your marriage. Once you reach consensus, express your commitment to adhering to this standard – either verbally or in writing.
2. Make a list of all that you, your children, your extended family and your church could lose if you failed to guard your marriage. Discuss this together.
3. Pray and ask the Lord to help you protect your marriage.
4. Review the suggestions in this chapter together and discuss which ones seem particularly relevant to you as a couple.

> *"Very few of us start out to disrupt marital intimacy. Sometimes we simply fail to establish it. Sometimes we fail to maintain it. More often we fail to protect it."*
>
> ~ GARY & MONA SHRIVER, AUTHORS OF THE BOOK *UNFAITHFUL*

CHAPTER 12

Dealing With Sexual Challenges

§

SOONER OR LATER, MOST COUPLES encounter some sexual challenges in their marriage. Those times call for shared ownership and mutual care and understanding. It will also take courage and perseverance from both of you.

Sexual struggles are frustrating, but we encourage you not to get stuck in a place of discouragement or thinking "this is how it will always be." As we have emphasized throughout this book, phenomenal sexual connection in your marriage is something you grow and develop. It is not a stagnant process, but rather one where you continually and sacrificially look for ways to strengthen – and in some cases, heal – your sexual bond.

Sexual struggles do not fix themselves. If you are not proactive in discussing these issues, then unhealthy patterns will become the norm, and satisfaction will decrease.

This chapter is not by any means exhaustive, but it will help you better understand some of the more common problems you may encounter. Hopefully, it also will heighten your awareness to these issues and other struggles so that you can limit the toll they will take on your marriage.

Common Female Sexual Challenges

Some female sexual challenges we have covered earlier in the book, including the following topics and their respective chapters:

* Poor body image (Chapter 5)
* Struggle with having an orgasm (Chapter 6)
* Low sexual desire (Chapter 8)
* Painful sex (Chapter 8)
* Decline in sex drive after birth of a baby (Chapter 10)

An additional topic to consider that greatly affects women:

Menopause

Menopause is the stage in a woman's life when she physically transitions out of her childbearing years. For some women, perimenopause (early menopause) can begin as early as her late thirties.

Typically, when a woman is between the ages of 40 and 50, ovulation (release of eggs) starts to decline. Production of the hormones progesterone and estrogen also decline. While a woman can experience a variety of effects of menopause, some of the more common ones are hot flashes, weight gain and vaginal dryness. Her emotions and sex drive may also fluctuate as her body adjusts to the changes in hormone levels.

In recent years, there has been more availability to what is commonly referred to as Hormone Replacement Therapy (HRT). The purpose of HRT is to minimize the symptoms of menopause. HRT involves taking estrogen alone or estrogen with the hormone progestin, the synthetic form of progesterone.

Health care professionals have differing views as to whether or not HRT is healthy. Some research shows that HRT increases a woman's risk for blood clots, strokes, cancer and other conditions. Other research suggests that short-term use of HRT may be a healthy way to deal with the negative effects of menopause.

As you approach menopause, we encourage you to read about menopause, as well as HRT, and talk extensively with your health care providers before deciding what is right for you.

Regardless of what you decide, no doubt menopause will affect your sexual intimacy. Don't assume your husband will intuitively understand the hormonal complexities of a woman's body. More than likely, the journey is as baffling for him as it is for you!

As you become educated about menopause, share what you are learning with your husband. From a sexual intimacy standpoint, you both may notice your increased vaginal dryness, which may make sex painful or difficult. Consider a quality artificial lubricant such as Sliquid®, which you can buy online.

Menopause doesn't have to spell the end for sexual intimacy in your marriage. As with other stages of life, this time in your marriage is another opportunity to be accommodating, to deepen your communication about sex and to find ways to draw closer together sexually.

Hormonal Imbalance

Age and other factors can cause an imbalance in a woman's hormone levels. In particular, a decrease in the hormones estrogen and testosterone may negatively impact a woman's sex drive. Our bodies produce other hormones as well, such as the thyroid hormone and melatonin, and an imbalance in these also may adversely affect a woman's life. Your doctor can test your hormone levels to determine if there is an imbalance. In some cases, there are treatment options that can decrease the imbalance and/or limit the symptoms.

COMMON MALE SEXUAL CHALLENGES
Below are three areas that men may encounter during their marriage.

PREMATURE EJACULATION (PE)
Some men find that their body responds to physical stimulation quicker than they, or their wife, desires. As a result, his enjoyment of intercourse is shortened – literally and figuratively – and the likelihood of bringing his wife to an orgasm during intercourse is reduced. The couple also may become dissatisfied in the limited time they have to enjoy the physical closeness during sex.

Ejaculatory control is a learned skill, and it may take some practice. First, you will need to learn what it feels like to approach your "point of no return." When you feel yourself approaching that point, stop thrusting and tighten and hold your pubococcygeus muscle (referred to as your PC muscle). Remember the Kegel exercises we recommended in Chapter 8? If you have been practicing these exercises on a regular basis, they will help you experience more intense feelings during ejaculation and can also help with overcoming PE.

You will need to stop thrusting, and your wife also will need to be still for a while. You may even need to withdraw from your wife's vagina, as you allow the arousal feelings to subside. Once that happens, take your time and use more gradual thrusting. You may need to repeat this several times as you learn how to control your sexual response. Don't become frustrated; rather, view it all as an opportunity for the two of you to better understand each other's bodies and the intensity of sexual feelings.

You or your wife may also help the process by gently but firmly squeezing under the base of your penis or under the ridge of the head of your penis, with your thumb and two fingers. This will help reduce your level of excitement, enabling you to extend your time of intercourse.

As a husband, you may find that using a condom can reduce your sensitivity to physical stimulation and help prolong your erection for a few minutes.

If premature ejaculation is an ongoing struggle, consider trying more foreplay, with particular focus on the wife's arousal. Use various forms of caressing and stimulation to bring her closer to orgasm before intercourse. It may help ease a husband's anxiety about "not being able to last" if he knows that his wife is incredibly close to orgasm as well.

IMPOTENCE OR ERECTILE DYSFUNCTION (ED)

At some time during a man's life, he is likely to experience one or more episodes of *impotence* – "the inability to have or maintain an erection." Impotence can be temporary or ongoing and may be due to a psychological, physical or medical cause, or as a consequence of stress, distraction, using pornography, or excessive alcohol consumption.

The process of having an erection involves a man's vascular, neurologic and hormonal systems. The quality of the marriage relationship also impacts it. In order to determine the root cause(s) of ED, evaluating each of these areas is necessary. Your doctor should be able to determine what is interfering with your body function. Fortunately, there are ways to successfully treat ED.

Having your first experience with impotence can be unsettling, but the key is to keep cool and don't get stressed about it. If you get anxious about your performance, that unnecessary anxiety may just become a self-fulfilling prophecy the next time.

If you have performance anxiety, consider how you view sex and if those thoughts are from God or other sources. God created sex and thinks it's wonderful. You need to get to that place of understanding as well.

Learn to relax and focus on your wife's love. Get to know each other so well that you lose any sense of awkwardness, embarrassment or shame when you are together. Discuss and resolve any issues that have formed an emotional wall between you. Get help from a Christian counselor, mentor or pastor, if necessary. Don't stay stuck where you are.

If you find you are distracted by thoughts about work demands or other struggles, then you may want to dig deeply into finding better work/life balance. Talk to your wife about outside pressures you may be having and ways the two of you can work toward alleviating some of those pressures.

A leading cause of erectile dysfunction among otherwise healthy men is using online pornography. Users often have a difficult time being turned on by their spouse after viewing an endless stream of erotic images. Real sex begins to feel like "bad porn." In these situations, the user needs to stop viewing pornography completely to allow his brain to rewire itself. This process can take up to 12 months.

We really can't emphasize open communication enough. It is not uncommon for a man who experiences impotence to then stop initiating sex and/or refuse the sexual initiation of his wife. This seeming lack of interest can leave her questioning whether her husband still finds her desirable. She then may withdraw from him out of fear of rejection. A downward spiral persists, leaving both of them sexually frustrated, emotionally wounded and increasingly unsure how to discuss the growing distance between them.

If you are impotent on an ongoing basis, the problem is physical in nature, and you need to discuss this issue with your doctor. You may be experiencing a side effect from a medication you are taking or have a hormone deficiency, nerve problem or poor circulation. Do not stop or change any medications without first talking to your doctor.

Fortunately, most underlying causes of impotence are treatable, so don't be ashamed or feel foolish and deprive yourself and your wife of a fulfilling sex life.

LOW TESTOSTERONE

A man's testosterone level can decline as he ages or has a health condition such as diabetes, obesity or a problem in his testicles. If your testosterone level goes below normal levels, you may experience decreased libido, erections that are less firm, loss of body hair, reduced muscle mass, feeling depressed or a decrease in energy. If you experience these symptoms, talk to your doctor to determine the root cause and to see if you should be tested for low testosterone, also known as "Low T" or hypogonadism.

Treatment options for Low T include topical gels, solutions or transdermal patches that are applied daily. Testosterone injections are another available form of treatment that your doctor may administer every one to two weeks. This is often the course of action if the couple is trying to get pregnant. Patients typically notice an improvement in their performance within a few weeks of starting treatment.

Testosterone treatment is not without adverse health risks, especially for men who have had certain forms of cancer, so be sure to consult your doctor before beginning any treatment regimen.

USE OF PORNOGRAPHY

While the use of pornography isn't just a problem for men, men are more frequently consumed by pornography's addictive nature than women are. For the purposes of defeating pornography in your life, we suggest that you consider pornography to be anything that triggers sexual thoughts or arousal that doesn't align with God's plan for you.

We like this working definition because it can help any person, who wishes to avoid being trapped by the addictive nature of pornography or break free from it, recognize material that he or she is becoming aroused by. If you use some vague definition, you will be distracted from the real issue that you need to address.

WHAT IS PORNOGRAPHY ADDICTION, AND HOW DO I IDENTIFY IT?
While there isn't official recognition of pornography addiction in the current edition of the Diagnostic and Statistical Manual of Mental Disorders (DSM-5), the following characteristics of other addictions may be useful for identifying where professional help is needed to address pornography use.

* *Neglecting responsibilities* at school, work, or home
* *Using porn under risky conditions* like at work or on work computers
* *Engaging in illegal activities* such as child porn, prostitution or rape
* *Ignoring problems* it is causing in your relationships with others
* *Developing a tolerance* and needing more deviant materials in order to have the same sexual effect
* *Using porn to relieve other symptoms* such as restlessness, anxiety, insomnia or depression
* *Losing control* over when porn is used and feeling powerless to change
* *Your life revolving around porn use*, thinking about porn and where to access it
* *Discontinuing activities that you used to enjoy,* such as hobbies, sports, and socializing, because of your porn use
* *Continuing to use porn* despite knowing its use is hurting you and your relationship

At a more personal level, here are some questions to consider:

* Do you have sexually explicit websites bookmarked on your computer?
* Have you participated in sexually related chats?

- Have you masturbated while on these sites?
- Have you accessed these websites from multiple computers?
- Do you hide what's on your computer, tablet or phone from others?
- Have you stayed up late in order to privately access sexual materials?
- Have you posted or downloaded any photos of a sexual nature?
- Do you cover your tracks by clearing your browsing history or creating elaborate folder systems that would be difficult for someone else to uncover?
- Do you use Internet porn as a personal reward or to get even with your spouse for neglecting you?
- Have you given out your contact info to others that your spouse would be upset knowing about?

As we have shared at various points in this book, pornography is devastating on many levels. There is *no* room for pornography in the sacred covenant relationship of marriage. Tragically, many people downplay pornography's negative impact because of society's growing acceptance of it and the ease at which it can be accessed.

We encourage you, however, not to underestimate the damage pornography use and addiction will have on your marriage. In Chapter 13, we give suggestions on overcoming the use of pornography.

Revitalizing a "Sexless Marriage"
The term "sexless marriage" is used to describe married couples who have sex less than ten times per year, yet are physically healthy

enough to have sex. This is more common in marriages than most people realize.

There are countless reasons why a couple might find themselves in this situation, and many couples need professional counseling or therapy. What we will address here is the case where you both desire to resume sexual relations and, while you may feel awkward about resuming sex, you both feel you are ready to revitalize the sexual part of your marriage.

A process that many couples have used to restart their sex life is called Sensate Focus.[1] This process is designed to help couples bond by getting in touch with their needs and becoming more aware of the sensations of giving and receiving touch that they enjoy.

SENSATE FOCUS – PHASE 1

1. The beginning of this process is the Non-genital Touch phase, which typically lasts from two to four weeks at your discretion. Schedule several times for this and find a comfortable place in your home where you can both be relaxed and uninterrupted. You may also wish to use candles and relaxing music to help create the right mood.

   During this phase, you can either wear loose clothing or be naked, as your comfort level increases. You may find it useful to have some gentle massage oils available for these sessions.
2. Take turns, either during a session or from one session to the next, giving each other a massage. Be careful not to touch the genital areas or your wife's breasts, and do not have intercourse during this phase.

3. Begin the process with your spouse lying face down for the first session. The following session he or she can lie face up and then alternate. Massage all of the non-genital areas from head to toe.

4. As you explore each other's body, focus your attention completely on the feelings you get when giving and receiving touch, as well as the closeness that you experience with each other. Provide feedback regarding what you enjoy verbally, with affirming sighs, or by placing your hand over your spouse's hand and guiding him or her.

5. Afterward, discuss how you each experienced touch during the session and share what you found enjoyable.

SENSATE FOCUS – PHASE 2

The second phase of this process is the Genital Touch phase, which lasts for at least two weeks, or longer if you desire a more gradual progression toward intimate touching.

1. At the start of this phase and for several sessions, incorporate gradually increased touching of the breasts, in addition to the massage areas that were included during phase 1.

2. When you both feel ready to proceed further, incorporate touching the areas around the genitals. In later sessions, incorporate touching the genitals themselves (your wife's clitoris and the entrance to her vagina or the head and shaft of your husband's penis). For genital stimulation, you may want to use a water-based lubricant, especially if a condom is being worn.

3. If you both agree, you may incorporate manual and/or oral stimulation into both your non-genital and genital touching. You may also consider using a vibrator at this time.

4. Finally, incorporate penetration, first with one of you on top and then the other. Start with minimal thrusting, and focus on enjoying the initial sensations of intercourse. In later sessions, you can incorporate more intense thrusting and experiment with different sexual positions in order to determine which positions are most comfortable and pleasurable for both of you.

The goals for this phase are to increase your awareness of increasing pleasure and how you each respond to different types of stimulation. Keep your focus off of striving to orgasm or any pressure of performing. Instead, concentrate deeply on pleasurable sensations of touch throughout the process. Doing so will minimize any performance anxiety, which will inhibit orgasm.

GOING DEEPER TOGETHER

1. How can you make your relationship more understanding, respectful, tender, playful and/or experimental?
2. If your spouse is experiencing one of the sexual challenges mentioned in this chapter, discuss ways that you can support and encourage him or her to get professional help in overcoming that challenge.

CHAPTER 13

Healing From Sexual Brokenness

As AUTHORS AND SEXUAL INTIMACY advocates, we are not naïve about the amount of sexual brokenness that many people have experienced.

Has sex in your past been marked by agony and ache? Are those encounters now diminishing the profound oneness you desire with the spouse you love? If so, we want you to know that we do not minimize your grief.

At some point, you will need to peel back the layers of pain so that you can move toward a healthier and more accurate perspective on sex. Often, gaining that healthier perspective will take the support of a Christian counselor or pastor with training in this area. You don't have to work through this alone.

Sexual brokenness happens when sex has been forced, coerced, or misused in any way apart from God's perfect and holy intentions. Sexual intimacy that is nurtured in its right context of marriage is a tender reflection of God's heart. On the other hand, when sin, shame and depravity enter the scene, sex becomes a destructive path to the pain of sexual brokenness.

Here are four areas we would like to briefly address.

225

SEXUAL ABUSE
Sexual abuse is the forcing of unwanted or improper sexual activity by one person on another, which may be accompanied by threats, coercion or the abuse of power or position.

Many women and men have been sexually abused in the past. Some were abused by close family members and friends, while others were abused by strangers, acquaintances or trusted adults (such as relatives, teachers, coaches, pastors or priests).

The damage left in the wake of this abuse is apparent and sometimes debilitating. When someone has been abused sexually, the abused person can find it excruciatingly difficult to view sex in a positive light once married. Viewing sex positively, though, is vital for a former abuse victim to have a healthy and fulfilling marriage. God did not design sex to be an optional part of marriage.

That being the case, it is in the best interest of the person who was sexually abused to seek healing through professional Christian counseling and other resources, and to work closely with his or her spouse to nurture authentic sexual intimacy.

PORNOGRAPHY
The discovery that one's spouse has been using pornography can be devastating. The sense of betrayal is often accompanied by the offended spouse wondering if he or she is somehow inadequate physically or sexually. These feelings are often unfounded.

Pornography use has a little to do with sex. It is often used by a person who is curious, feels inadequate with a real intimate relationship, has ongoing unresolved conflict with his or her spouse or feels trapped and powerless in some area of life.

A key step in breaking free from pornography is identifying the root cause. It is then wise to take a multi-faceted approach to breaking this habit, including:

1. Establishing an accountability team, meeting with them regularly and giving them complete authority to ask you any question necessary to assess your progress toward sexual purity
2. Confessing your sin to God and your spouse with complete repentance, humility and honesty, and investing in strengthening your marriage
3. Renewing your mind and body by spending time each day in Bible study and prayer, and getting proper rest, exercise and nutrition
4. Removing sources of temptation or removing yourself from entertaining them (This should include Internet filtering software and elimination of any media that results in sexual arousal.)
5. Developing the habit of removing yourself from tempting situations, especially when you are bored, lonely, angry, stressed or tired

It is extremely unlikely that the male porn user will be able to break this habit on his own. It will take a team approach, with the wife's primary role being prayer, care and encouragement.

We realize that men aren't the only ones who struggle with pornography use and addiction. One of the fastest growing groups of pornography users today is women, who now make up about 30 percent of users.

Sadly, many women who use pornography were introduced to it or encouraged to use it by their intimate partners. For other women, their use of pornography is closely related to codependency rooted in a childhood of abuse or having an absent parent who left her feeling inadequate or unworthy of real love.

Women who use pornography often do so in order to satisfy the demands or desires of their partner. This leads them to feeling even more inadequate and unworthy of love. As you can see, this cycle eventually poisons marital intimacy in a marriage and will continue to do so until the underlying issues are addressed through counseling.

More on this topic can be found in *The Solution for Marriages* book (coauthored by Jeff) and other books recommended on our website, http://pursuitofpassionbook.com.

ADULTERY

Adultery is most often defined as a married person's having sexual contact with a person who is not his or her spouse.

While a common assumption is that a marriage can never survive adultery, there are numerous examples of couples who have marriages that not only survive, but go on to be quite strong.

If you and/or your spouse have committed adultery, we urge you *not* to immediately see divorce as your only option. There is great hope of the marriage surviving if the offending spouse repents, the offended spouse extends grace and both commit to work together on rebuilding trust and intimacy.

This is rarely, if ever, a smooth or quick process. Nearly all couples who have restored their marriage after adultery will contend that it is a heart-wrenching journey that should include the help of a professional marriage counselor and/or mentor.

Some things that need to take place for healing to have a chance are:

* The offending spouse must be willing to take full ownership for his or her actions and immediately cut off *all* contact with the person with whom he or she committed adultery.
* The offending spouse must honestly and fully answer any questions that his or her spouse has now or in the future, such as what happened, for how long, when, where, and why. That said, it would be wise for the offended person to only ask questions that will be helpful to their healing.
* The cause(s) for the infidelity need to be uncovered and measures put in place to address them so that this doesn't happen again.

A husband and wife are each responsible for nurturing their marriage. When they don't do this, one or both of them are likely to be more susceptible to committing adultery. We believe strongly, though, that one spouse's carelessness to nurture the marriage is not an excuse for the other spouse to have an affair. Ultimately, adultery is a decision, and the person who decides to be unfaithful is responsible for that decision.

Restoring sexual intimacy after adultery does not happen immediately. In addition, if sexual relations were involved, it is wise for both the husband and wife to get tested for STDs before resuming sex and to use a condom for at least six months, until negative verification of STD test results have been received. When trust has been compromised and broken, rebuilding it to the point of being able to have sex again will take time.

Through the process of healing and building healthier communication patterns as well as establishing boundaries that protect the marriage, a couple can experience renewed intimacy on all levels.

While it takes an average of two years of counseling and hard work for a couple to recover from the pain of adultery, we can't define how long such a process would take in your marriage. Each case is unique. What we can say is that ultimately, the timetable for healing must be up to the offended person, often in consultation with their counselor.

Numerous resources are available that are designed specifically for married couples wanting to recover from adultery. These may include books, counseling, seminars and/or weekend intensives.

Many people would say that adultery is not limited to sexual contact, but also includes "emotional adultery." This is when a married person shares intimate emotional connection that is romantic in nature with someone other than his or her spouse. The participants don't get physical, but the marriage still suffers because of the emotional betrayal.

While some married couples that face this issue may think it is the beginning of the end of their relationship, we know for a fact that countless marriages do survive emotional adultery. As is the case with physical adultery, restoring trust and intimacy after emotional adultery will take the effort of both spouses. It also will be crucial for them to establish more secure boundaries that protect their marriage.

ABORTION

I (Julie) remember clearly a women's retreat I attended several years ago. While the topic of abortion was not on the agenda, we all soon discovered that it was on God's agenda. I believe God wanted to use this retreat to speak hope and healing into the lives of several Christian women who had had abortions in their past. Spontaneously and courageously, many of these women stepped forward to share with agony and transparency about the abortions they previously had.

The body of believers is not untouched by the deep woundedness of abortion, and it is likely that when you sit in church or in any gathering of Christians, you are with some women who have had abortions – but have never revealed that fact to their Christian friends.

Christian women, in fact, may be more likely to go to great lengths to keep secret their past abortion, for fear of being judged and marginalized by other Christians.

The truth of God, however, is that if a woman asks for forgiveness and repents of her abortion, God does indeed forgive her.

Sadly, some women believe that their past abortion destines them to sexual intimacy that will never be fulfilling. In other words, if they experience sexual struggles in their marriages, they believe it is because of their past sin of abortion and that God is punishing them. This perspective, though, does not mirror God's heart and His truth about forgiveness. Also, His Word is clear that He desires that sexual intimacy be a safe and fulfilling haven in a marriage. Nowhere does God indicate that some married people are more entitled to this fulfillment than others.

If you have had an abortion, that sin is not beyond the reach of Christ. Fortunately, there are resources designed specifically for women who have had abortions and then want to embrace God's forgiveness – as well as going on to gain a right perspective on healthy sexual intimacy.

Finding Healing

Ultimately, the deepest level of healing and restoration comes from God. We have all been wounded by our sins and the sins of others. We strongly encourage you to begin your own personal healing by receiving forgiveness from God by coming into a personal relationship with Him through faith in Jesus Christ.

You can learn more by reading and applying the material in Addendum 2, speaking to your pastor or emailing us at help@ pursuitofpassionbook.com.

CHAPTER 14

Other Resources

§

WE TRUST THAT YOU HAVE found this book helpful in your marriage. Here are some resources that may be helpful for some couples with needs or interests beyond what we have addressed.

Please note that while the websites and resources listed below may be useful to you, we do not have any control over what they offer now or may offer in the future. Therefore, we do not necessarily endorse their content or product offerings. Use your own discretion and discernment regarding the suitability of these websites for your marriage.

BREAKING FREE FROM PORNOGRAPHY & SEX ADDICTION
For Men
Every Man's Battle http://everymansbattle.com
Faithful and True http://faithfulandtrueministries.com
Setting Captives Free http://settingcaptivesfree.com

For Women
Whole Women Ministries http://wholewomenministries.com

RECOVERING FROM ADULTERY
Hope and Healing Ministries http://hopeandhealing.us

CHRISTIAN MARRIAGE BLOGS ON INTIMACY
Engaged Marriage http://www.engagedmarriage.com
The Generous Husband http://the-generous-husband.com
The Generous Wife http://www.the-generous-wife.com
Hot, Holy and Humorous http://www.hotholyhumorous.com
Intimacy In Marriage http://intimacyinmarriage.com
To Love, Honor and Vacuum http://tolovehonorandvacuum.com
The Marriage Bed http://themarriagebed.com
One Extraordinary Marriage http://www.oneextraordinary-marriage.com
One Flesh Marriage http://www.onefleshmarriage.com
The Romantic Vineyard http://www.theromanticvineyard.com
Unveiled Wife http://unveiledwife.com

INTERNET ACCOUNTABILITY & FILTERING SOFTWARE
X3 Watch http://www.x3watch.com/
Covenant Eyes http://www.covenanteyes.com

SEX AIDS & ACCESSORIES
Covenant Spice http://covenantspice.com
Three Passions Gifts http://threepassionslingerie.com

CHRISTIAN SEX THERAPISTS & COUNSELORS

Finding a Christian counselor or sex therapist is important in order to get professional help that is biblically sound. This will take some careful investigation and evaluation on your part. While we do not necessarily endorse these organizations, here are some that may be able to help you get started. You may also want to talk to your pastor and/or doctor.

American Board of Christian Sex Therapists
1325 Satellite Blvd NW, Suite 102
Suwanee (Atlanta area), Georgia, USA
(678) 389-7311

Building Intimate Marriages
Suwanee, Georgia, USA
(770) 822-4505
http://intimatemarriage.org/therapy-with-bim/sex-therapy.html

Focus on the Family
Colorado Springs, Colorado
(855) 771-4357
http://focusonthefamily.com
Christian therapists are available by phone, Monday – Friday, 6:00 a.m. - 8:00 p.m.

The Intimacy Counseling Center
Dr. Douglas Rosenau
Atlanta, Georgia, USA
(770) 813-1544
http://intimacycounseling.com

Passionate Commitment
Dr. Clifford and Joyce Penner
Pasadena, California, USA
(626) 449-2525
http://passionatecommitment.com

Potential Health Benefits From Sex

§

"A good marriage at age fifty predicted positive aging at eighty. But, surprisingly, low cholesterol levels did not."

~ GEORGE VALLIANT, MD, HARVARD MEDICAL SCHOOL

THERE ARE SEVERAL HEALTH BENEFITS that couples may be able to benefit from by having sex with their spouse regularly. Here are some that we have found in the research literature and numerous other publications.

Sex:

* Releases endorphins, those feel-good hormones which increase a person's sense of overall happiness and wellbeing. (University of Colorado at Boulder)
* Burns about 100 calories per 30 minutes, which when combined with a healthy lifestyle can help you lose weight and improve your self-esteem.
* Lowers stress levels by releasing dopamine and oxytocin which counters the stress hormone, cortisol and enables

you to sleep better. (Berman Women's Wellness Center) Oxytocin has also been found to enhance your desire for your spouse, enhance trust and reduce physical pain – including arthritis and yes, headaches too. (Beverly Whipple, Rutgers University)

* Increases your respiration rate which increases the oxygen supply to your cells
* Boosts testosterone and estrogen levels, which are needed to strengthen your muscles and bones
* Reduces your diastolic (resting) blood pressure
* Boosts your immune system by increasing immunoglobulin A (Wilkes University)
* Three or more times per week helps you look younger by releasing estrogens, which fill out your skin and reduces fine lines. (Royal Edinburgh Hospital)
* Can improve your heart health and reduce heart attack and stroke risk. DHEA is released during orgasm and can reduce the risk of heart disease. (New England Research Institute & British Royal University)
* Reduces the risk of prostate cancer (JAMA)
* Helps you maintain strong bladder and bowel function
* Helps regulate a woman's hormone levels and menstrual cycle
* Produces healthier sperm, a consideration for couples seeking to get pregnant
* Reduces feelings of depression by releasing chemicals that boost serotonin, helping you feel better (American Archives of Sexual Behavior)

If great marital sex was a patented drug, it would certainly be a blockbuster!

Developing Your Relationship With God

§

THROUGHOUT THIS BOOK, WE HAVE referenced biblical principles and spoken often about God's intentions for your marriage and sexual intimacy. For some of you, these references made perfect sense. For others, it may have left you wondering, "Why should I care about God's intentions? Does God really care about sex and my marriage?"

These questions point to an important story. A *big* story. A story that's much bigger than each of us!

God has a design and a purpose for our lives. That's why He put us here. Discovering that and then living it out is the reason for our existence. Missing that purpose is tragic, and we want to encourage you to carefully consider what we are about to share because it will make all the difference in your life and marriage.

God has a wonderful plan and a purpose for your life and your marriage. But there's a core problem we all have that separates us from His plan and purpose.

Sin.

When we do anything out of selfishness, anger, greed or bitterness, we hurt ourselves, others and God. We've all done this, and our sin has taken us to a state of brokenness – personally, relationally and spiritually.

Our brokenness is painful, so we look for solutions to remove the pain. Typically human solutions are based on what *sounds* right. But ultimately, since those "solutions" don't deal with our core problem, we can't escape our brokenness.

But there is a real solution available to us. God's solution!

God's solution starts with our repenting of our sin. *Repentance* means "turning away from our selfishness, pride, anger, etc. and doing the opposite." Then we need to apply God's Word to our life. We do this by trusting in Jesus Christ's payment for our sins on the Cross, yielding our life to Him as Lord, and seeking to live our life in accordance with His Word, the Bible.

When we make this commitment, God's Holy Spirit comes into our life and gives us the power to continue living out God's design or purpose for our life.

The process looks like this.

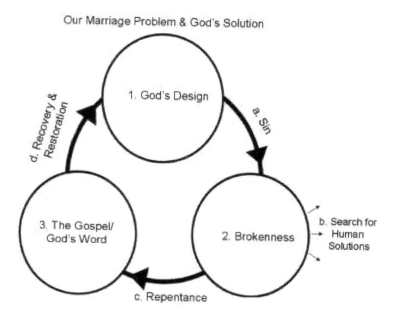

SOURCE: Dr. Jimmy Scroggins

(Note: The numbering and lettering that follows corresponds to the diagram above.)

1. **God's Design: God loves you and created a special plan or design for your life (and marriage)...but,**
   a. Sin: Your sin has separated you from God, who is holy and righteous.

   "For all have sinned and fall short
   of the glory of God."

   (ROMANS 3:23)

   "Your sins have cut you off from God."

   (ISAIAH 59:2)

> *"Whoever shall keep the whole law, and yet*
> *stumble in one point, he is guilty of all."*

(JAMES 2:10)

2. **Brokenness: Our sin has brought us to a state of brokenness (pain, quarrels, abuse, suffering, etc.).**
   b. Search for Human Solutions: Our rational mind tells us to pursue happiness using human ideas or "solutions." We keep trying new things or working harder, but that doesn't work.

> *"There is a way that appears to be right,*
> *but in the end it leads to death."*

(PROVERBS 14:12)

> *"For the wages of sin is death...."*

(ROMANS 6:23A)

   c. Confession and Repentance: The solution to our problem begins with confession of our sin and repentance. *Confession* means "that we acknowledge that what God says about our sin is true." *Repentance* means "to turn away from our sins and to turn toward God."

> *"If we confess our sins, He is faithful*
> *and just and will forgive us our sins and*
> *purify us from all unrighteousness."*

(1 JOHN 1:9)

3. **The Gospel:** The good news (or Gospel) is that Jesus Christ loves you and has already paid the penalty for your sins. He is God's *only* provision for our sin and solution for our brokenness. Believe it!

   Your good works won't save you; Jesus had to be sacrificed in your place.

> *"For by grace you have been saved through faith,*
> *and that not of yourself, it is the gift of God,*
> *not of works lest any man should boast."*

(EPHESIANS 2:8-9)

> *"...the Lord has laid on Him [Jesus]*
> *the iniquity of us all."*

(ISAIAH 53:6B)

> *"God made him [Jesus] who had no sin*
> *to be sin for us, so that in him we might*
> *become the righteousness of God."*

(2 CORINTHIANS 5:21)

> *"God demonstrates his love towards us, in that*
> *while we were yet sinners, Christ died for us."*

(ROMANS 5:8)

Jesus is the only way.

> *"...for this reason I was born, and for this I came into the world, to testify to the truth. Everyone on the side of truth listens to me."*

(JOHN 18:37)

> *"I am **the** way **the** truth and **the** life; no one comes to the Father but through me."*

(JOHN 14:6)

d. Recovery and Restoration: By receiving Jesus Christ into your life and committing to follow Him as your Lord, you can recover and restore God's plan and design for your life and spend eternity in Heaven.

> *"But as many as received Him, to them He gave the right to become children of God, even to those who believe in his name."*

(JOHN 1:12)

> *"God has given us eternal life, and this life is in the Son. He who has the Son has life; and he who does not have the Son of God does not have life. These things I have written to you who believe in the name of the Son of God, that you may **know** that you have eternal life."*

(1 JOHN 5:11-13)

"Behold I stand at the door and knock;
if anyone hears my voice and opens
the door, I will come in to him."

(REVELATION 3:20)

"I tell you, now is the time of God's
favor, now is the day of salvation."

(2 CORINTHIANS 6:2)

To receive Jesus as your personal Lord and Savior and to begin the process of recovering and restoring God's design for your life and marriage, sincerely pray the following prayer:

Dear God,

I confess that I have sinned against You and that my sin has left me in a place of brokenness. I realize that I can't save myself from this condition by my own works. I acknowledge that Jesus Christ died on the Cross, to take the judgment that I deserve, and then rose from the dead in fulfillment of the Scriptures. I invite Jesus Christ to come into my life now, to be my personal Lord and Savior. Help me to live for You each day, as I put my trust in Him.
Amen.

When you make your decision to follow Jesus, please share that with your spouse, a friend and your pastor. They will be greatly encouraged to know that and will be able to rejoice with you. Welcome into the family of God!

NEXT STEPS IN YOUR SPIRITUAL JOURNEY

After you have made the decision to follow Jesus Christ as your Lord and Savior, the next step is to learn how to live a victorious Christian life. Here are some steps that we recommend that you take.

1. Get connected with a church that teaches the Bible and has a worship style that you like. If you know someone who is a mature Christian, ask him for suggestions. Otherwise, you might need to check out a few churches before you find the right one for you.

2. Become a part of a Bible study group or discipleship program. This is where you will learn the fundamentals of the Christian faith, get many of your questions answered and live out your faith authentically and transparently.

3. Read your Bible each day, beginning in the New Testament or the Gospel of John.

4. Pray and ask God to help you to understand His Word and to help you see areas of your life that need to change. Then turn from those areas in your life that displease God.

5. Get baptized as a believer. This is the biblical model, taught by Jesus in Matthew 28:19-20. Baptism is one way you can publically declare you are a new creation and a follower of Jesus.

6. Find a place to serve others through the ministries of your church and learn how to share your faith with others. There is a lot of work to be done in sharing the good news about Jesus with others who haven't yet come to know Him.

NOTES

Chapter 1: Why a Book on Sex for Christians?

1. Mark Driscoll, MenMakers Conference, Edinburgh, Scotland, 2007.

2. Lester Sumrall, *60 Things God Said About Sex (South Bend,* Ind.: LeSea Publishing Company, 1981) 14.

3. James Brundage, *Law, Sex, and Christian Society in Medieval Europe* (Chicago: University of Chicago, 1987) 89.

4. Ibid., pg. 7.

5. David Hunter, "Sexuality, Marriage, and the Family." Cambridge History of Christianity 2: 589, 2007.

6. Alastair Heron, ed., "Towards a Quaker View of Sex - A*n Essay by a Group of Friends,*" London Annual Meeting of the Society of Friends, 1963.

Chapter 2: A Biblical View of Sex and Marriage

1. David Popenoe and Barbara Dafoe Whitehead, *Should We Live Together? What Young Adults Need to Know About Cohabitation Before Marriage.* Rutgers University, 2009.

2. Tim Gardner, *Sacred Sex: A Spiritual Celebration of Oneness in Marriage* (Colorado Springs: WaterBrook Press, 2002) 8.

Chapter 4: Preparing for Your Honeymoon and Marriage

1. Portions of this chapter are adapted from *The Solution for Marriages*, Murphy and Dettman, 2011.

2. Adapted from *Family Life*, Weekend to Remember Conference Manual (1985): 86.

3. "Dissatisfied, Ladies? Tips to Reach the Big O." MSNBC, 11. 2. 2007.

Chapter 5: Desire and Arousal

1. Michael Metz, *Features of Enduring Desire and Satisfying Couple Sex*, Society for the Scientific Study of Sexuality, 2011.

2. Nancy Etcoff et al, "The Real Truth About Beauty: A Global Report," 2004.

3. David Stoop and Jan Stoop, *When Couples Pray Together* (Ventura, Cal: Regal Books, 2000) 7.

4. Jim Burns, *Creating an Intimate Marriage* (Ada, Mich.: Bethany House, 2007) 161.

5. Those parts of a person's body that are especially sensitive to arousing stimulation by touch, licking and so forth. These areas may include the neck, breasts, earlobes, navel, the inside crease of the elbow, thighs, genitals, etc.

Chapter 6: Orgasm – God's Gift for You and Your Marriage

1. Adapted from Dictionary.com

2. The "G-spot" was named for Dr. Ernst Grafënberg, a German gynecologist who researched this area of a woman's body in the 1940s.

Chapter 7: Talking Together About Sex

1. Tim Gardner, *Sacred Sex: A Spiritual Celebration of Oneness in Marriage* (Colorado Springs: WaterBrook Press, 2002) 82.

2. http://www.netdoctor.co.uk/sex_relationships/facts/orgasmtrouble.htm

3. Rick Johnson, *The Marriage of Your Dreams: A Woman's Guide to Understanding Her Man* (Ada, Mich.: Revell, 2012) 105.

Chapter 8: Honest Answers to Real Questions About Sex

1. Alcohol has been found to be a sexual disinhibitor for women. Studies indicate that women may experience increased sensations of pleasure during orgasms because alcohol relaxes the mind and allows women to be more sexual. If you choose to use alcohol, use it in moderation.

2. The term "love language" was popularized by Dr. Gary Chapman in his book, *"The Five Love Languages."* They are words of affirmation, acts of service, physical touch, quality time together and gifts. For more information, go to http://5lovelanguages.com

Chapter 10: Maintaining Intimacy as New Parents

1. Pamela Stock, *Parents Magazine*, October 2004, http://www.parents.com/parenting/relationships/staying-close/marriage-after-baby/.

2. Sherry Rauh, "Will Baby Strengthen or Strain Your Marriage?", WebMD.

3. Ibid.

Chapter 12: Dealing with Sexual Challenges

1. The Sensate Focus technique was introduced by Masters and Johnson, and is intended to increase awareness of the husband and wife's personal needs and responses to touch.

About the Authors

JEFF & GLYNIS MURPHY

AT THE AGES OF 23 and 19 respectively, Jeff married Glynis, the woman he had been praying for. After a few years of wedded bliss, their marriage began a downward spiral as a result of being inadequately trained in the skills necessary for a successful marriage, the demands of a budding career, the arrival of two children, and their own selfishness and immaturity. A growing sense of frustration and isolation infected their hearts and home.

It was out of this despair that Jeff and Glynis began their quest to learn how to be successfully married – a journey that has now continued for nearly 30 years. While deeply studying the topic of marriage and developing new marriage skills, they began sharing their story with other couples in small group studies and investing their time in marriage ministry through their local church. Marriage ministry and couple mentoring has been a part of their lives ever since. In 2011, Jeff co-authored the highly acclaimed book, *The Solution for*

Marriages: Mentoring a New Generation, which is being used to train marriage mentors around the world.

Jeff holds a Bachelors degree in Engineering and a Masters degree in Business Administration. After 35 years in the healthcare field, he retired from an executive management position at Johnson & Johnson in order to devote more time to helping couples build awesome marriages, serving as a personal mentor to men in several states and as a friend and advisor to pastors.

Glynis holds a degree in Dietetics and worked as a nutrition counselor prior to retiring. She now enjoys mentoring couples with Jeff, encouraging other women individually and spending fun times with their grandchildren.

Jeff and Glynis have two grown children.

Jeff and Glynis also enjoy encouraging their global audience each day with marriage tips on Twitter as @marriagementor, @PursuitOPassion and on Facebook at facebook.com/pursuitofpassionbook.

RANDALL & JULIE SIBERT

With tremendous gratitude for the way God crosses paths, Randall and Julie met in 2001 when they became neighbors.

Having previously been married, Julie had endured the pain

of a divorce she neither asked for nor wanted. When she and her toddler son moved into a basement apartment in the house next to Randall's home, she was doubtful another relationship was on the horizon. Turns out, it wasn't on the horizon, but just across the yard. Randall, though, had his own doubts. He had wanted to be married for quite some time, but at age 35, had nearly given up on the possibility. Enter God, stage right!

Randall and Julie began a courtship not long after meeting and married in 2003. They embarked on journey that continues to remind them of God's provision and patience.

Because of some of the intimacy struggles in her first marriage, Julie was determined that sex would be a sacred and nurtured part of her marriage to Randall. Neither of them have ever regretted such a decision!

Out of a God-driven desire to encourage wives in their marriages, Julie began writing and speaking on sexual intimacy. She strives to shed light and hope into this area of marriage that is wrought with difficulties, yet rich with potential for profound connectedness.

Randall and Julie live in Omaha, Nebraska, where they are doing all they can to keep up with their sons, Mitchell and Bradley.

Julie blogs about sex regularly at http://IntimacyInMarriage.com and tweets irregularly at @Intimacy4Life. When she's not driving the carpool, you can find her enjoying ridiculously overpriced coffee.

§

It has been our pleasure helping guide you in your journey to deeper intimacy. We trust that you have found this book to be helpful in equipping you to enjoy all that God intends for your marriage.

Please help us spread the word by recommending this book to other couples who may be settling for less than God's best, and by posting your comments online.

Thank you and may God bless you and your marriage as you enjoy His wonderful gift!

Made in the USA
San Bernardino, CA
23 December 2016